FARMER
RECIPES AND STORIES
FROM THE LAND

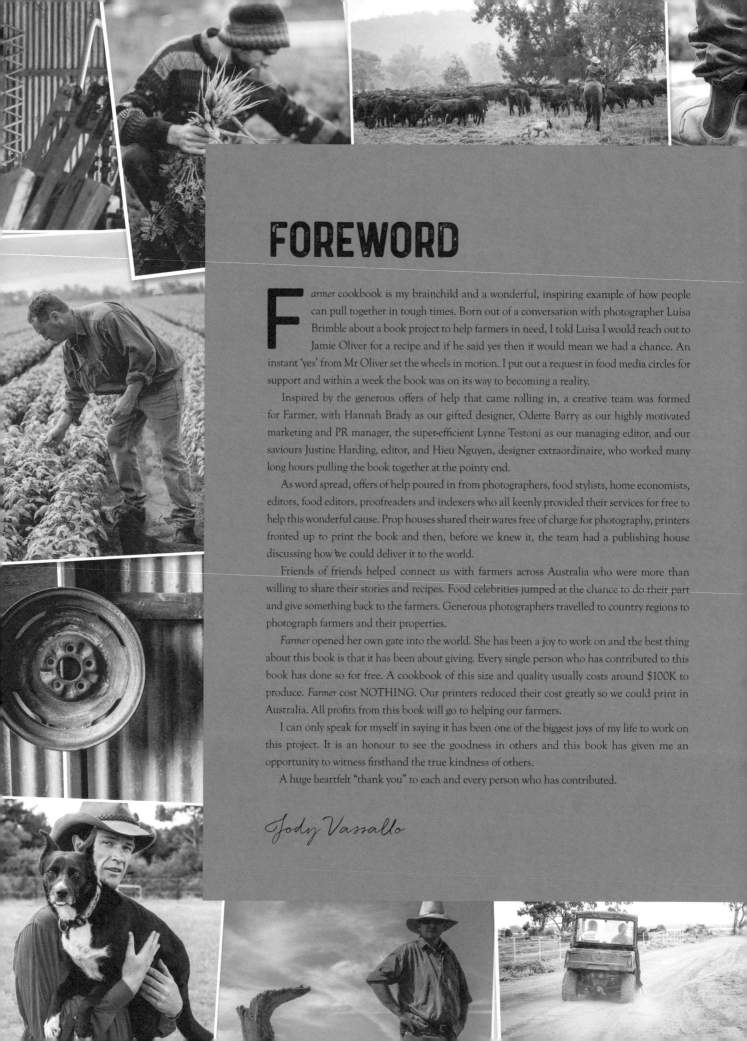

FOREWORD

Farmer cookbook is my brainchild and a wonderful, inspiring example of how people can pull together in tough times. Born out of a conversation with photographer Luisa Brimble about a book project to help farmers in need, I told Luisa I would reach out to Jamie Oliver for a recipe and if he said yes then it would mean we had a chance. An instant 'yes' from Mr Oliver set the wheels in motion. I put out a request in food media circles for support and within a week the book was on its way to becoming a reality.

Inspired by the generous offers of help that came rolling in, a creative team was formed for Farmer, with Hannah Brady as our gifted designer, Odette Barry as our highly motivated marketing and PR manager, the super-efficient Lynne Testoni as our managing editor, and our saviours Justine Harding, editor, and Hieu Nguyen, designer extraordinaire, who worked many long hours pulling the book together at the pointy end.

As word spread, offers of help poured in from photographers, food stylists, home economists, editors, food editors, proofreaders and indexers who all keenly provided their services for free to help this wonderful cause. Prop houses shared their wares free of charge for photography, printers fronted up to print the book and then, before we knew it, the team had a publishing house discussing how we could deliver it to the world.

Friends of friends helped connect us with farmers across Australia who were more than willing to share their stories and recipes. Food celebrities jumped at the chance to do their part and give something back to the farmers. Generous photographers travelled to country regions to photograph farmers and their properties.

Farmer opened her own gate into the world. She has been a joy to work on and the best thing about this book is that it has been about giving. Every single person who has contributed to this book has done so for free. A cookbook of this size and quality usually costs around $100K to produce. *Farmer* cost NOTHING. Our printers reduced their cost greatly so we could print in Australia. All profits from this book will go to helping our farmers.

I can only speak for myself in saying it has been one of the biggest joys of my life to work on this project. It is an honour to see the goodness in others and this book has given me an opportunity to witness firsthand the true kindness of others.

A huge heartfelt "thank you" to each and every person who has contributed.

Jody Vassallo

CONTENTS

INTRODUCTION

Farming in Australia is as old as its people. On some of the earth's oldest crust people have harvested seeds, tubers and fruits, as well as the meat they needed, for longer than anyone really knows.

As I crisscross our dry land the scale of the current drought is deeply confronting. Farming is such a huge part of our national psyche. With over 50% of our land under agricultural production it's not only a $60 billion industry that's under threat but the future of some of the farmers who help feed us and the world.

Beef, mutton and wheat lead our farm exports today but in some parts, farmers have had to handfeed their animals and watch the fields turn to dust. Every Australian can surely see that we're in the grip of a slow-moving catastrophe and it is farm families that feel it the most.

The Millennium drought in the 2000s was the longest dry stretch in recorded history, with 9 years of dismal autumn rains so crucial for the cropping season. With just 57mm on average, autumn 2018 looks like the driest since the 1902 Federation drought.

Looking ahead, climate change can only exacerbate the complexity of the challenges faced by Australia's farmers trying to produce food in the driest inhabited continent. The changes occurring everywhere are dramatic.

By 2100 one-third of all living species may be gone. Watch our birds on the wing because of 10,000 extant species, 7000 are in drastic decline. Take a long walk through a forest and drink deep of its beauty because 50,000 of the world's 250,000 kinds of plants are expected to disappear over the next few decades.

You don't have to tell farmers about species extinction as they stare at their fallen animals.

It's the farmers and earth scientists who now call in unison for a national drought policy. Handouts are not what they seek, but a thoughtful hearing and a government response that matches the devastation. Supplementing funds to keep cattle and sheep alive does not address the bigger need for an adequate policy that recognises the vastness of the great southern drying and the urgent need for a strategy to keep decreasing moisture in the ground.

Like many who contribute to this book in support of the farmers, we have in our own family histories the memory of ancestors who lost almost everything and yet kept farming.

At a time like this we stand on common ground. We're a community and we're with you, farm families. Stay strong like an old iron bark.

Jeff McMullen

BREAKFAST

TIM & SOPHIE HANSEN

DEER FARMERS, ORANGE, NSW

Tim and Sophie Hansen's deer are calm as they free-range on the slopes of Mount Canobolas, 25 minutes west of Orange, because they are bred and handled in a holistic respectful manner. Animal welfare is a priority for the couple, who have been farming for more than 15 years. Theirs is a vertically integrated farm and agribusiness. That means they do everything from breeding the deer to processing and then marketing the meat through their business, Mandagery Creek Venison.

Nothing goes to waste – the meat is sold into high-end restaurants both at home and overseas, and the antlers and skins are turned into homewares by Tim's sister, Penny. Her brand, 1803 Artisan Deer, stocks deer leather purses and bone-handled implements.

Tim has been farming deer since 2002, while Sophie left the city and joined him a few years later. She says she appreciates the privilege of raising their children in such a beautiful space and it hasn't taken her long to become totally sold on the lifestyle.

"I never expected this to be my life but the space, challenges, independence and satisfaction of running our own business and being caretakers for this beautiful property are all now in my blood," she says. "Tim manages most of the operations on our property. That said, I love heading out early in the morning or late in the afternoon to check water, feed, stock. That 'golden hour' makes even the dustiest paddock look beautiful!"

A typical day, according to Tim, starts with the kids getting on the bus for school when the work day begins. "For me that means doing the rounds of the farm, checking fences, stock, feed and water," he says. "Then it's a bit of time in the office taking and filling orders, organising transport or making a few sales calls and, depending on the time of year, more work out on the farm. This could be moving stock, fixing or moving fences, putting in forage crops or cutting silage. As I'm sure is the case for most farmers, there's no such thing as a typical day here. Every day is different according to the weather, what the deer are up to and what orders I need to fill or meet."

In tough times, Tim takes time out to ensure weekends are dedicated to family. Whether it's bike riding, picnicking, sharing a movie or taking off for a rare trip to the coast to breathe some sea air, he says these little circuit-breakers help them stay positive.

350G MIXED FRESH BERRIES (RASPBERRIES,
    STRAWBERRIES AND BLUEBERRIES)
3 PEACHES, CUT INTO WEDGES
⅓ CUP (75G) CASTER SUGAR
1 TABLESPOON FRESH ORANGE JUICE
1 STRIP ORANGE RIND
1 VANILLA BEAN, HALVED LENGTHWAYS,
    OR 1 TEASPOON VANILLA BEAN PASTE

BUCKWHEAT CRUNCH
1 CUP (200G) BUCKWHEAT GROATS
1 CUP (25G) PUFFED BROWN RICE
2 TABLESPOONS LINSEEDS
PINCH OF GROUND CINNAMON
PINCH OF GROUND CARDAMOM
1 TEASPOON SEA SALT
¼ CUP (60ML) PURE MAPLE SYRUP

HONEY YOGHURT
1½ CUPS (390G) GREEK-STYLE PLAIN YOGHURT
2–3 TABLESPOONS HONEY

SOPHIE HANSEN'S

roasted stonefruit with buckwheat crunch & honey yoghurt

SERVES 4–6

1 To make the buckwheat crunch, preheat the oven to 180°C. Line a 30 x 20 x 5 cm baking tray with baking paper. Put all the ingredients on the tray and mix well. Bake for 20 minutes, until golden and crunchy, stirring halfway through cooking. Allow to cool, then store in a screw-top jar or an airtight container.

2 While the buckwheat crunch is cooling, put the berries, peaches, sugar, orange juice and orange rind in a bowl. Scrape in the seeds from the vanilla bean, or add the vanilla bean paste. Gently toss to combine.

3 Take two 60cm lengths of baking paper and lay one on top of the other to make a cross. Pour the fruit into the centre, twisting the ends of the paper together to hold it in place. Tie firmly with kitchen string and place the parcel on a baking tray. Bake for 20 minutes.

4 Meanwhile, to make the honey yoghurt, put the yoghurt in a bowl. Swirl the honey through the yoghurt.

5 To serve, place the fruit parcel on a plate, with a bowl of buckwheat crunch and the honey yoghurt.

My youngest years were on bush blocks as my dad, Jack, was from Branxton and my mum, Joyce, was from Singleton in the Hunter Valley of NSW. My understanding of what farmers go through came from stories handed down by my kin. My mother was a very independent young woman and rode her bicycle from property to property, cutting the ladies' hair. Like many country women she was enterprising, self-confident and exuded strength. I have an indelible memory of wandering through the paddocks with her looking for wild blackberries and mushrooms, which inspired my simple recipe for brunch in the bush. **JEFF MCMULLEN**

mixed mushroom sauté

SERVES 4

TIPS

Pile the mushrooms on the toast and allow the juices to drench the plate.
For a heartier meal (that my dad would call the Branxton Brunch), add roasted tomatoes, poached eggs and your favourite country sausage.

50G BUTTER, CHOPPED

300G PORTOBELLO MUSHROOMS, SLICED

250G BUTTON MUSHROOMS

125G PORCINI MUSHROOMS, SLICED

2 GARLIC CLOVES, SLICED

10 SPRIGS LEMON THYME (OR SAGE OR PARSLEY)

TOASTED SOURDOUGH BREAD, TO SERVE

1 Melt the butter in a large frying pan over medium heat. Fry the mushrooms and garlic, stirring, for about 7 minutes.

2 Reduce the heat to low and add the lemon thyme. Cover the pan to help retain the mushroom juices. Cook for a few minutes until the mushrooms are tender and juicy.

3 Serve the mushrooms from the pan, accompanied by the toasted sourdough.

1 CHORIZO SAUSAGE, DICED

4 EGGS

1 TEASPOON SALT

4 SOFT CORN OR FLOUR TORTILLAS, WARMED

1 AVOCADO, SLICED

¼ CUP (60G) SOUR CREAM

¼ CUP (25G) FINELY GRATED PARMESAN

HOT SAUCE, FRESH CORIANDER LEAVES,
    PICKLED JALAPEÑOS AND LIME WEDGES, TO SERVE

I am a city boy. To be more specific, I am a beach boy. However, through my job I've been extremely lucky to have spent time on the land, meeting farmers, talking with producers and getting 'hands on' all across our country. Having this small connection to our food and our farmers is more important than one might think. It demands respect. It makes you recognise that every time a plate of food hits your table, hours and hours of back-breaking and often selfless work has gone into getting that food into your mouth. Farming is not easy, it's rarely glamorous and more often than not, it's overlooked. We all need to thank our farmers, our producers and our growers, because without them, nothing would be possible. **HAYDEN QUINN**

chorizo breakfast tacos

SERVES 2 (MAKES 4)

TIP

I love smoky chipotle hot sauce for my breakfast tacos.

1 Add the chorizo to a frying pan and cook over low heat, stirring, until the fat renders and the chorizo is crisp. Drain the oil into a bowl.

2 Whisk the eggs and salt with 2 tablespoons water. Pour into the pan with the chorizo and cook for 30 seconds, using a wooden spoon to gently push the mixture around the pan, until the chorizo is incorporated and the eggs are just cooked.

3 Fill the warm tortillas with the chorizo and egg mixture. Top with the avocado, sour cream and parmesan.

4 Drizzle your favourite hot sauce over the tacos. Scatter with coriander leaves and jalapeños, and add a squeeze of lime juice to serve.

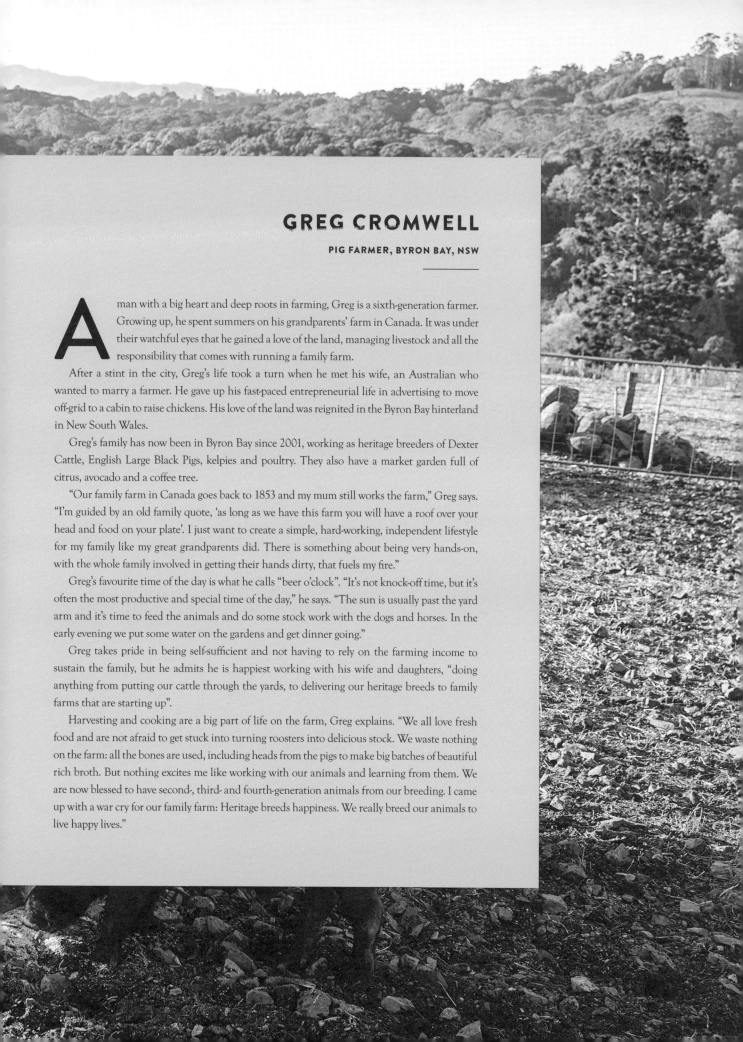

GREG CROMWELL

PIG FARMER, BYRON BAY, NSW

A man with a big heart and deep roots in farming, Greg is a sixth-generation farmer. Growing up, he spent summers on his grandparents' farm in Canada. It was under their watchful eyes that he gained a love of the land, managing livestock and all the responsibility that comes with running a family farm.

After a stint in the city, Greg's life took a turn when he met his wife, an Australian who wanted to marry a farmer. He gave up his fast-paced entrepreneurial life in advertising to move off-grid to a cabin to raise chickens. His love of the land was reignited in the Byron Bay hinterland in New South Wales.

Greg's family has now been in Byron Bay since 2001, working as heritage breeders of Dexter Cattle, English Large Black Pigs, kelpies and poultry. They also have a market garden full of citrus, avocado and a coffee tree.

"Our family farm in Canada goes back to 1853 and my mum still works the farm," Greg says. "I'm guided by an old family quote, 'as long as we have this farm you will have a roof over your head and food on your plate'. I just want to create a simple, hard-working, independent lifestyle for my family like my great grandparents did. There is something about being very hands-on, with the whole family involved in getting their hands dirty, that fuels my fire."

Greg's favourite time of the day is what he calls "beer o'clock". "It's not knock-off time, but it's often the most productive and special time of the day," he says. "The sun is usually past the yard arm and it's time to feed the animals and do some stock work with the dogs and horses. In the early evening we put some water on the gardens and get dinner going."

Greg takes pride in being self-sufficient and not having to rely on the farming income to sustain the family, but he admits he is happiest working with his wife and daughters, "doing anything from putting our cattle through the yards, to delivering our heritage breeds to family farms that are starting up".

Harvesting and cooking are a big part of life on the farm, Greg explains. "We all love fresh food and are not afraid to get stuck into turning roosters into delicious stock. We waste nothing on the farm: all the bones are used, including heads from the pigs to make big batches of beautiful rich broth. But nothing excites me like working with our animals and learning from them. We are now blessed to have second-, third- and fourth-generation animals from our breeding. I came up with a war cry for our family farm: Heritage breeds happiness. We really breed our animals to live happy lives."

crepes with bacon

**MAKES
ABOUT 22 CREPES**

TIP

For the crispy bacon, I suggest using the biggest roasting tin you have. Better yet, have two non-stick pans going that you can crank the bejesus out of with some big heat – the hotter the better.

4 LARGE EGGS

1½ CUPS (375ML) MILK

1½ CUPS (225G) PLAIN FLOUR

¼ TEASPOON SALT

125G SALTED BUTTER

20G UNSALTED BUTTER, SOFTENED

CRISPY BACON, TO SERVE

1   Pour the eggs and milk into a blender and blend until combined. Add the flour and salt. Blend on high speed until smooth, pausing once or twice to scrape down the side of the blender. Strain the batter into a jug and stand at room temperature for 30 minutes.

2   Melt the salted butter in a small saucepan over medium–high heat, then cook for 3–5 minutes, until the butter has the aroma of toasted nuts. Watch carefully as the butter can burn quickly. Skim off any foam that rises to the top. Allow the butter to cool slightly, then stir into the batter. The batter should be the consistency of thickened cream; thin it with a little more milk, if needed.

3   Place a small crepe pan or frying pan over medium–high heat. Add a little of the unsalted butter, swirling it over the base of the pan until it stops bubbling. Pour in enough batter to coat the base of the pan. Quickly tilt the pan so the batter is evenly spread over the base and a little up the side of the pan. Immediately pour any excess batter back into the jug.

4   Cook for 1–2 minutes, until the centre of the crepe is set and the bottom is lightly browned. Turn and cook for another 30 seconds, until the centre is firm and the edges are lightly browned. Transfer to a cooling rack. Repeat with the remaining batter. Once cool, stack the crepes between sheets of baking paper to prevent sticking. Serve with the crispy bacon.

RED KELPIE

WORKING DOGS

"Red Dog, that's me. I'm an Aussie dog with an Aussie name. My owner called me Red Dog, 'cos that's exactly what I am. I'm a red kelpie and I'm bred to be a farmer's right-hand man. Not all kelpies are red. Some are black and tan, others are jet black and quite a few have a big white blaze down their chest. You might even come across cream ones, but they always look really dirty if they're working dogs. Me, I'm a multipurpose dog. I can work with sheep, cows and pigs – and I'm loved by my family.

Us kelpies are pretty serious dogs. We can be shy and fairly suspicious. Don't be surprised if we don't come running up to you for a pat. That's not really our thing unless we know you and even then, we're fairly cautious. Kelpies are really smart, and our brains need constant stimulation. Our purpose in life is to work and we enjoy nothing more than a day of mustering. We love to run and can run up to 40 kilometres a day, rain, hail or shine. It's my job to keep the mob under control. My owner Greg has shown me neat tricks, but often I think I know more than he does about mustering sheep and cattle. We're a pretty intuitive lot and can get the animals in line just by being near them.

Our job is to move cattle or sheep from one paddock to another. Often this takes hours and requires my full attention. I need to listen carefully to what I'm being told to do. If I don't then boy, do I get an earful! Usually there are a few of us kelpies helping to move the stock. There will be one at the back, one at the side and one up front. I prefer working with sheep, but they can be pretty dumb. Often they get jammed up like cars in traffic. When this happens, I jump on their backs and run across to the sheep up the front, nip them on the ears and tell them to get a move on. Sometimes I'll even have a little kip on their backs if we're waiting to move them onto a truck.

I've got a pretty good life. Most of my days are spent outdoors on our big property and on a day off, Greg and his daughters take me and the horses to the beach for a run. Greg loves his daughters and don't get me wrong, I love my pups too, but I was happy to see the back of those feeding days. I've had four litters of pups. First I had four pups, then the next year it was six and then the last time there were ten. My owner says I did a great job with the little ones, but I prefer working with sheep. Greg's daughters kept pups from two of my litters, so now Bailey and Marley work with me. They're quick as lightning and know how to herd with compassion.

I know a lot of city folk think they'd like to own a kelpie, but we're not really city dogs. Unless you like to run an awful lot, we'd be bored to tears and probably start trouble. I went to the city once and it wasn't really my thing. All the dogs there seemed to like sitting at cafes or just laying around in the sun. They'd have a fit if they saw what I did in a day."

1 LARGE ZUCCHINI, GRATED

1 TEASPOON SEA SALT

300G FRESH CORN KERNELS
  (2 TO 3 CORN COBS)

6 GREEN ONIONS, FINELY CHOPPED

¼ CUP (5G) FINELY CHOPPED
  FRESH FLAT-LEAF PARSLEY LEAVES

2 TABLESPOONS FINELY CHOPPED
  FRESH DILL

2 EGGS, LIGHTLY BEATEN

¼ CUP (60G) SOUR CREAM

½ CUP (75G) UNBLEACHED PLAIN FLOUR

1 TEASPOON BAKING POWDER

1 TEASPOON GROUND NUTMEG

COCONUT OIL, FOR FRYING

100G FETTA

⅓ CUP (55G) ALMONDS, ROASTED, SMASHED

AVOCADO SALSA

2 AVOCADOS, DICED

1 TABLESPOON LIME JUICE

1 TABLESPOON EXTRA VIRGIN OLIVE OIL

Visiting my local farmers' market to pick up fresh, seasonal produce is the highlight of my week. We are so grateful for the farmers who grow our food. In this wholesome, high-fibre, 'all-day breakfast' dish, the fritters are matched with a creamy avocado and lime salsa, salty fetta cheese and crunchy roasted almonds. The fritters are great as they are, or you can add a hit of protein with a soft poached egg and some crispy bacon. **JANE GROVER**

sweet corn & zucchini fritters

MAKES 10
_____

1 Preheat the oven to 120°C. Combine the zucchini and salt in a colander or sieve. Set aside to drain while you prepare the other ingredients.

2 To make the avocado salsa, combine the avocado, lime juice and olive oil in a bowl. Season with salt and pepper.

3 Drain the zucchini, squeezing out any excess moisture. Transfer to a large bowl and add the corn kernels, green onion, herbs, egg, sour cream, flour, baking powder and nutmeg. Mix thoroughly. Season with salt and pepper.

4 Lightly grease a large frying pan with the coconut oil. Place over medium heat and cook the fritters in batches, adding ¼ cup (60ml) of batter for each fritter and spreading it out to an 8cm round. Cook for 2 minutes, then turn and cook for another 2 minutes, until golden brown. Place the fritters on a baking tray, loosely cover with foil and transfer to the oven to keep warm while you cook the remaining fritters.

5 Serve the warm fritters with the avocado salsa, crumbled fetta and smashed almonds.

200G STREAKY BACON, CHOPPED

2 TABLESPOONS FINELY CHOPPED
   FRESH ROSEMARY LEAVES

2 TABLESPOONS CHOPPED
   FRESH THYME LEAVES

3 GARLIC CLOVES, CRUSHED

3½ CUPS (525G) SELF-RAISING FLOUR

125G UNSALTED BUTTER, CHOPPED

1 CUP (250ML) BUTTERMILK

1 CUP (100G) FINELY GRATED PARMESAN

2½ CUPS (250G) GRATED SHARP CHEDDAR

1 EGG, WHISKED

CULTURED BUTTER

400G CRÈME FRAÎCHE

When I think of country cooking, I think of generous portions, fresh ingredients and great baking. Scones are simple and timeless, and this version celebrates all that comes from the land. From great butter and buttermilk, to rich cheeses, fresh herbs and smoky bacon, these scones represent the great variety and quality of Australian produce. Scones and tea is a warm welcoming gift I've enjoyed at many farms in Australia. These savoury scones can even be enjoyed with a cold beer – how Aussie is that? And they're even green and gold... WARREN MENDES

bacon, cheddar & herb scones with quick cultured butter

MAKES 12

1 Preheat the oven to 200°C. Line a baking tray with baking paper.

2 Place the bacon in a cold frying pan over medium heat. When the fat starts to render, cook, stirring often, for 4–5 minutes, until crisp. Add the herbs, garlic and some pepper. Cook, stirring, for 1 minute. Remove from the pan and set aside to cool.

3 Add the flour and butter to a food processor. Process until fine crumbs form. Transfer to a large bowl and mix in the buttermilk, parmesan, 2 cups of the cheddar and the bacon mixture, and season with salt.

4 Turn the mixture out onto a lightly floured surface and knead lightly to form a soft dough. Roll the dough out to a 3.5cm thick round and use a 6cm floured cutter to cut it into rounds. Place the scones close together on the baking tray. Re-roll any left-over dough and cut it into rounds. Brush the scones with the egg and scatter the remaining cheddar over the top. Bake the scones for 25 minutes, until golden and cooked through.

5 Meanwhile, to make the cultured butter, beat the crème fraîche with an electric mixer until it turns to butter. Season with salt. Serve with the scones.

As a kid, picking mushrooms, catching mullet, trapping yabbies and feeding the chooks were all part of my everyday life on the farm in Brooweena, about four hours north-west of Brisbane. School was obviously compulsory, but shoes were not. It was quite the rural experience. I have never taken my childhood for granted – growing up on the farm with an incredible amount of freedom and connection to all that is real and all that could be imagined. I had my own BMX track, tree house and ninja hide-out. **JASON ROBERTS**

beetroot, pear & pumpkin seed bircher

SERVES 4

2 FIRM PEARS, GRATED

2 CUPS (200G) ROLLED OATS

1 CUP (250ML) BEETROOT JUICE

1 CUP (250ML) ALMOND MILK

1 CUP (260G) COCONUT YOGHURT,
    PLUS EXTRA TO SERVE

¼ CUP (50G) CHIA SEEDS

½ CUP (50G) PUMPKIN SEEDS,
    CRUSHED

125G FRESH BLUEBERRIES,
    PLUS EXTRA TO SERVE

PUMPKIN SEEDS, TO SERVE

1   Combine all of the ingredients in a large jar or mixing bowl and mix well. Cover and refrigerate for 6 hours or overnight.

2   Serve the bircher muesli with extra fresh blueberries, pumpkin seeds and a little coconut yoghurt.

1 CUP (150G) ORGANIC PLAIN FLOUR

1 CUP (150G) ORGANIC SELF-RAISING FLOUR

100G BUTTER, CUT INTO CUBES

1 EGG

¾ CUP (185ML) MILK

FILLING

6 EGGS

200ML CREAM

PINCH OF GROUND CAYENNE PEPPER
   (OPTIONAL)

GRATED CHEESE, SLICED MUSHROOMS,
   SAUTÉED BACON, HALVED CHERRY
   TOMATOES, SLICED GREEN ONIONS,
   TO TASTE

We have a big lake in front of our farmhouse and every year we have a family of black swans living there. We go out and check on them every day and see the babies. We watch their flying lessons, and we know we've made a safe place for them. The land and nature are telling us that what we are doing is the right thing, because the animals want to live here. **WENDY JOHNSTON**

breakfast mini quiches

MAKES 12

---

1 Add the flours, butter and a good pinch of salt and pepper to a food processor. Pulse until the mixture resembles breadcrumbs. Tip the egg into a measuring jug and pour in enough milk to make 1 cup (250ml). Whisk together.

2 Tip most of the egg mixture into the food processor and process until the mixture starts to form a ball around the blades. Add the rest of the egg mixture or a little more flour to make a soft, pliable dough.

3 Turn the pastry out onto a lightly floured surface. Form into a ball. Wrap in plastic wrap and rest in the fridge for 1 hour or overnight.

4 Preheat the oven to 180°C. Roll out the pastry on a floured surface and cut out 12 rounds to line a 12-hole muffin pan.

5 To make the filling, whisk the eggs, cream and cayenne with some salt and black pepper in a large bowl. Add the grated cheese and other filling ingredients of your choice. Divide the mixture among the pastry cases and sprinkle with a little more grated cheese.

6 Bake the quiches for 12–15 minutes, until set and golden brown. Serve.

As fifth-generation farmers, we believe there is a deep connection between what we eat and who we are. Our farm means more to us than just land and a crop – it is our heritage and our future. We are in the fortunate position of growing an abundance of avocados. Avo smash is one of those healthy treats that you want to eat, and it is something our whole family eats nearly every day – for breakfast and lunch. **JULIA FOYSTER**

'next level' avo smash

SERVES 4

1 TABLESPOON BALSAMIC VINEGAR
1 TEASPOON MAPLE SYRUP
4 SLICES GOOD-QUALITY SOURDOUGH BREAD
2 RIPE AVOCADOS, THINLY SLICED
2 RIPE TOMATOES, DICED
60G CRUMBLED FETTA
DUKKAH, TO SERVE

1 Combine the balsamic vinegar and maple syrup. Set aside.
2 Toast or grill the bread until golden. Place a sliced avocado half on top of each bread slice and roughly smash.
3 Season the tomato with salt and pepper and gently toss. Place on the avocado.
4 Top with the crumbled fetta, dukkah and a drizzle of the maple–balsamic to take your avo smash to the next level.

SHANE HICKEY

DAIRY FARMER, KYOGLE, NORTHERN NSW

———

A fter his video calling supermarkets and shoppers to arms on one-dollar milk went viral, Shane Hickey has created a platform agitating for change.

A rriving at Shane's farm there's a smell in the air, and Shane quickly addresses it – it's the smell of very welcome rain. It's a beautiful smell and everyone's happy and relieved, even the birds. But Shane is cautious; the bureau is saying this might be it. Normally you would need sunglasses to look at the fluorescent green grass, but right now the farm is prickly paddocks of brown.

Shane and his brother took over the 100-year-old farm in 1994 from their parents, who had worked the land for 15 years. Now, Shane and his wife, Julie, work the farm, along with their kids. It was initially a dairy farm, but the brothers have explored both dairy and beef on the 200-acre slice of heaven in the shadows of the Border Ranges.

For Shane, this is paradise and he brims with pride. "It's magnificent. Over the hill here, you have six valleys to Mount Woodenbong, and to the north it's the Border Ranges – you can't get much better than this." The farm is in a special spot and while some of Australia is wrestling a drought, this little spot is partial to a drop of rain.

"The weather here is pretty unpredictable. The BOM (Bureau of Meteorology) can't really help us with predictions, but we have the water tank that just about guarantees our water supply from the creek, so we do all right," he says. "I chose this lifestyle because I wanted to be around for my kids and I wanted to bring them up on the land, but I think the supermarkets and end-customers need to stop and think about the choices they're making and the lasting impact it's going to have for generations to come."

In an age where resources are at the fingertips of supermarket shoppers, Shane wishes that more Australians understood the value of food – that they would know where it came from, appreciate what's involved in producing it, and understand that by undervaluing food, we're creating an underclass of food producers and reducing the quality of what arrives on our plates.

HOT CHOCOLATE

4 CUPS (1 LITRE) MILK

200G GOOD-QUALITY DARK CHOCOLATE,
   ROUGHLY CHOPPED

½ CUP (55G) COCOA POWDER

2 TABLESPOONS BROWN SUGAR

1 TEASPOON VANILLA EXTRACT

1 CINNAMON STICK

FRENCH TOAST

4 EGGS

1¼ CUPS (310ML) MILK

¼ CUP (60G) COCONUT SUGAR

2 TEASPOONS GROUND CINNAMON

2 TEASPOONS GROUND NUTMEG

1 TEASPOON VANILLA EXTRACT

1 GOOD-QUALITY SOURDOUGH LOAF,
   THICKLY SLICED

100G BUTTER

MAPLE SYRUP OR AUSTRALIAN PURE
   HONEY, TO SERVE

BLUEBERRIES, TO SERVE

SHANE HICKEY'S

sunday morning hot chocolate & french toast

SERVES 4

TIPS

We prefer using full-cream milk (with the cream on top if possible), but use whatever type you prefer.
You can serve the French toast with sliced banana instead of the blueberries.

1   To make the hot chocolate, combine the milk, chopped chocolate, cocoa, brown sugar, vanilla and cinnamon stick in a saucepan. Heat over low heat until the milk just starts to simmer (keep an eye on it as it can boil over quickly). Cook, stirring occasionally, for 10 minutes, until the chocolate has melted and the mixture is very smooth. Remove from the heat, then reheat gently before serving.

2   To make the French toast, whisk the eggs, milk, coconut sugar, spices and vanilla in a shallow dish. Working with a couple of pieces at a time, dip the bread into the egg mixture, making sure it soaks up some of the liquid.

3   Melt a chunk of butter in a large frying pan over medium heat. Cook the soaked bread for about 3 minutes on each side, until golden brown. Repeat with the remaining bread and egg mixture, melting more butter as needed.

4   Serve the warm French toast with maple syrup or honey and blueberries, with the hot chocolate on the side.

MAINS

SAM & STEVE GRIMA

VEGETABLE FARMERS, HORSLEY PARK, NSW

For Sam and Steve Grima, farming has always been what they do and who they are. The brothers like the idea that they feed people's families, and that when customers buy their vegies, their customers in turn are feeding the Grima family.

Sam says that one of the best things about his job is the satisfaction he gets from planting crops, seeing them grow and taking them to market for sale. "It's a job that makes me proud," he says. "Growing vegies is intrinsically rewarding and satisfying."

Located in a green belt on the outskirts of Sydney, Sam and Steve and their wives have been working the farm for 32 years, growing a variety of vegetables for markets and restaurants. Their parents established the farm around 1960, with Sam taking over at the age of 20 and Steve joining him after he left school.

Sam says his family gave him a choice about what he wanted to do with his life, but for him, it was always going to be farming. "It just was one of those things," he says. "It gets into your blood, and if you're working and you enjoy it, why would you do anything else?"

While their parents grew the standard Aussie vegies, the brothers found a niche in the last 10 years or so, growing speciality vegetables for the restaurant business and farmers' markets - coloured carrots, cabbages and beetroot, and mini leeks.

Sam is the first to admit that establishing the farm was hard work, particularly in the early days, but says the rewards far outweigh the pain. "It's not a bad life, but you've got to put in the effort," he says. "It's relentless, but at the end it can be very rewarding."

Those early years were about developing the property and investing in the infrastructure, Sam explains. "You have to put the money back into the business, and we had a lot of years when we didn't have money for ourselves. You would go and build a shed, and that's big money, and you'll need the concrete, and then you need a couple of quad bikes and then you need another tractor. Farming is like that - it's very hungry. And, as soon as you think you have got there, your tractor needs replacing."

And while there can be tough days, such as the current dry spell, the brothers like to keep their eyes on the long haul.

"You've got to look at it as a cycle," Sam says. "You've got to try and prepare for those tough days, and you've got to manage it. We cut down when it doesn't rain and we haven't got as much water as we want."

"I love farming. I always wanted to be a farmer," adds Steve. "I think in this day and age, farmers are appreciated more than they used to be. Once upon a time we were on the bottom. We've always copped the low prices and the weather, but I think nowadays, people have a relationship with farmers, and that's a really good thing."

SAM GRIMA'S

beetroot & rocket salad

SERVES 4–6

TIP

You can use the leaves of the baby beetroot if they are fresh. Reduce the rocket to 60g and add 60g baby beetroot leaves.

1 BUNCH BABY BEETROOT, SCRUBBED, TRIMMED

1 BUNCH GOLDEN BEETROOT, SCRUBBED, TRIMMED

2 TABLESPOONS OLIVE OIL

500G KENT PUMPKIN, SEEDS REMOVED, CUT INTO LARGE WEDGES

300G SWEET POTATO, PEELED, THICKLY SLICED

1 BUNCH HEIRLOOM CARROTS, SCRUBBED, TRIMMED

120G BABY ROCKET LEAVES (SEE TIP)

250G FETTA, CRUMBLED

1 CUP (120G) WALNUTS, TOASTED

2 TABLESPOONS EXTRA VIRGIN OLIVE OIL

LEMON WEDGES, TO SERVE (OPTIONAL)

1 Preheat the oven to 220°C. Line two large baking trays with baking paper. Place all of the beetroot on one of the trays. Season with salt, drizzle with half the olive oil and cover the tray with foil. Arrange the pumpkin, sweet potato and carrots on the second tray. Drizzle with the remaining olive oil and season with salt. Roast all of the vegetables for 20 minutes, until tender. Set aside to cool.

2 Peel the beetroot and cut in half. Arrange the rocket on a platter and top with the pumpkin, sweet potato, carrots and beetroot. Sprinkle with the fetta and walnuts. Drizzle with the extra virgin olive oil and serve with lemon wedges on the side.

BLUE CATTLE DOG

G'day, I'm Stubbs. I'm a breed of dog known by lots of different names, including cattle dog, Australian cattle dog and Australian heeler. Because of my blue-mottled coat, I'm also called a blue heeler, but there are red-mottled cattle dogs out there as well.

Sure, all blue heelers are bred especially for cattle herding, but I have to say that I'm a natural when it comes to being a working dog. I came to my owner, Tara Lee, without any training at all, but I take my farm duties in outback Queensland very seriously. The best days are the days I get to race around the property and go out mustering, helping to find cattle and bringing them back to the yards. I'm also handy when it comes to weaner tailing – I'm pretty good at educating weaners, blocking them up and putting them back in their spot if they try to buck out from the mob.

I'm not really into being bored and Tara Lee reckons I have too much energy, but all cattle dogs do. My ears are always upright, waiting for important instructions. That's just the way it is when you're a super-smart bluey.

I might be small, but don't let my size fool you. I'm brave when I need to be. Even though I'm a bit wary of strangers (it's best not to try to take me by surprise), I've stood up to some of the biggest bulls in a herd. But that's not all I can do – I have a few tricks up my blue-mottled sleeve. I can shake hands, beg, wave, lay down and roll over if you ask me to. I've even been asked to be a dog model because people reckon I'm photogenic (you can catch me in the 2018 Akubra Calendar). I'm too busy on the farm to do any more modelling, though.

We have a special bond, Tara Lee and me. I'm her trusty sidekick and wherever she goes, I go too. She knows she can always count on me.

5 SMALL OR 10 BABY BEETROOT, SCRUBBED,
   TRIMMED
50G BUTTER
1 TABLESPOON EXTRA VIRGIN OLIVE OIL,
   PLUS EXTRA TO SERVE
1½ TABLESPOONS APPLE CIDER VINEGAR

1 TABLESPOON RAW SUGAR
1 SHEET FROZEN PUFF PASTRY, JUST THAWED
150G DANISH FETTA, CRUMBLED
1 HANDFUL OF FRESH MINT LEAVES
BABY ROCKET, TO SERVE

A good farmer has to be a skilled craftsperson. There's a lot to know, from soil chemistry and soil physiology to biology, as well as understanding business and markets. It's a demanding job, but it's very satisfying. **FRASER BAYLEY**

beetroot tarte tatin

SERVES 4

1   Preheat the oven to 180°C.
2   Cook the beetroot in a saucepan of boiling water for about 20 minutes, until tender when pierced with a small knife. Drain and cool slightly, then slip off the skins. Cut in half or into thirds if larger.
3   Heat the butter and olive oil in a frying pan over medium heat. Stir in the vinegar and sugar, then add the beetroot and gently toss until well coated. Transfer to a 20cm pie dish, ensuring the beetroot pieces are sitting cut side up.

4   Trim the pastry sheet to fit the pie dish, then lay it over the top of the beetroot, tucking it in around the edge of the dish. Bake the tart for 20–25 minutes, until the pastry is puffed and golden brown. Set aside for 10 minutes to cool slightly.
5   Place a large serving plate over the pie dish and invert the tart onto the plate. Scatter the fetta and herbs over the tart, season with pepper and drizzle with a little olive oil. Serve the tart with baby rocket.

¼ CUP (60ML) OLIVE OIL, PLUS EXTRA
    TO SERVE

3 SMALL EGGPLANT, CUT INTO CHUNKS

2 STALKS CELERY, SLICED

1 LARGE RED ONION, CHOPPED

2 LARGE GARLIC CLOVES,
    THINLY SLICED

1 BUNCH FLAT-LEAF PARSLEY, LEAVES
    AND STEMS CHOPPED SEPARATELY

PINCH OF SALT

2 RED CAPSICUMS, CUT INTO CUBES

5 RIPE TOMATOES, CHOPPED

¼ CUP (60ML) VINEGAR

1 TABLESPOON SUGAR, PREFERABLY RAPADURA

¾ CUP (130G) GREEN OLIVES, PITTED, CHOPPED

⅓ CUP (60G) RAISINS

2 TABLESPOONS SALTED CAPERS, RINSED,
    DRAINED

¼ CUP (40G) PINE NUTS, LIGHTLY TOASTED

My connection to the land is the opportunity to live at Glenmore
House, nestled into the Razorback Range just south-west of Sydney.
It's old dairy farming country and we're lucky that our neighbours
continue to milk twice a day... their cows and farm are our 'borrowed
landscape'. Although we have 30 acres of land and a few head of
cattle ourselves, I mostly get my hands into the soil via the garden
we've made here over 30 years. **MICKEY ROBERTSON**

sicilian caponata

SERVES 4

_____

TIP

The caponata tastes great
after a few hours, and even
better the next day.

Adapted from an original
recipe by Anastasia Georgeu
for Seasonal Cooking at
Glenmore House.

1 Heat half the olive oil in a large frying pan
over high heat. Cook the eggplant, stirring,
for 10 minutes, until golden. Remove from
the pan.

2 Heat the remaining olive oil in the same frying
pan over medium–high heat. Cook the celery,
onion, garlic, parsley stems and salt, stirring,
for 5 minutes, until softened. Add the capsicum
and cook for 5 minutes. Return the eggplant to
the pan. Add the tomato, vinegar and sugar.
Cook for 2–3 minutes, until the tomato starts
to soften.

3 Stir in the olives, raisins and capers. Simmer
for 10 minutes, until the vegetables are tender.
Add a good lug of olive oil and set aside to cool.
Sprinkle with the parsley leaves and pine nuts
just before serving.

1KG BEEF BRISKET, CUBED

½ CUP (75G) PLAIN FLOUR

100ML VEGETABLE OIL

8 PEARL ONIONS, HALVED

2 STALKS CELERY, CUT INTO 2CM DICE

1 CARROT, CUT INTO 2CM DICE

4 GARLIC CLOVES, CRUSHED

2 CUPS (500ML) VEAL STOCK

200ML PALE ALE

1 SHEET PUFF PASTRY

1 EGG YOLK, WHISKED

It's no secret that Aussies love a meat pie. I've had pies of various types on my menus for years, particularly in the colder months. **MATT MORAN**

beef & ale pie

SERVES 4

1 Preheat the oven to 150°C.

2 Coat the beef cubes in the flour and season with salt and pepper.

3 Place a frying pan over high heat. Add half the oil and swirl to coat. Fry the beef in two batches until sealed. Remove from the pan and set aside.

4 Heat the remaining oil in a large ovenproof saucepan over medium heat. Add the onions, celery, carrot and garlic. Cook for 3 minutes. Add the beef, then pour in the veal stock and ale (the beef should be just covered). Bring to the boil, skimming off any fat that rises to the surface.

5 Cover the saucepan and transfer to the oven. Bake for 1 hour, until the beef is tender. Remove from the oven. Season with salt and pepper and transfer to a small ovenproof dish.

6 Increase the oven temperature to 200°C. Cut the pastry sheet into a circle a little larger than the ovenproof dish. Place on top of the dish, crimping the edge. Make a couple of vents in the middle and brush the pastry with the egg yolk.

7 Place the dish on a baking tray and bake the pie for 10 minutes, until the pastry is puffed and beginning to brown. Reduce the oven to 170°C and bake for a further 10 minutes, until golden.

2 TABLESPOONS OLIVE OIL

1.5KG (4) BEEF OSSO BUCCO PIECES

1 ONION, CHOPPED

1 LEEK, TRIMMED, CHOPPED

4 STALKS CELERY, CHOPPED

100G FLAT PANCETTA, CUT INTO LARDONS

6 GARLIC CLOVES, THINLY SLICED

4 ANCHOVY FILLETS

½ TEASPOON DRIED CHILLI FLAKES

2 CUPS (500ML) DRY WHITE WINE

4 CUPS (1 LITRE) VEAL OR BEEF STOCK

SOFT SEMOLINA OR POLENTA, TO SERVE

BROCCOLI GREMOLATA

200G BROCCOLI FLORETS

1 CUP (20G) FLAT-LEAF PARSLEY LEAVES,
  CHOPPED

2 GARLIC CLOVES, FINELY CHOPPED

1 TABLESPOON FINELY GRATED LEMON ZEST

¼ CUP (60ML) OLIVE OIL

Each year I have the honour of being involved with the *delicious.* Produce Awards, which allows me direct contact with producers who don't always have a voice in the wider food community. It is also a time when the message really gets through about just how hard it is to be working and trying to earn a living off the land. **KIRSTEN JENKINS**

osso bucco in bianco

SERVES 4
————

1 Preheat the oven to 150°C.

2 Heat the oil in a large ovenproof saucepan over medium heat. Add the osso bucco pieces and cook for 2 minutes on each side, until well browned. Remove from the pan and set aside.

3 Add the onion, leek, celery, pancetta, garlic, anchovies and chilli flakes to the pan. Cook for 7 minutes, until the vegetables are tender. Pour in the wine and bring to the boil. Cook for 8 minutes, until the liquid has slightly reduced. Stir in the stock.

4 Return the osso bucco to the pan and bring to the boil. Cover the saucepan and transfer to the oven. Cook for 3 hours, until the meat is falling off the bone.

5 Meanwhile, to make the gremolata, blanch the broccoli in a saucepan of boiling water for 1 minute, until just tender. Drain and refresh under cold running water. Transfer the broccoli to a food processor. Pulse until roughly chopped. Combine with the parsley, garlic, lemon zest and oil. Season with salt and pepper.

6 Remove the osso bucco from the pan and keep warm. Place the pan over medium heat. Bring to the boil and cook for 10 minutes, until the sauce has reduced and thickened.

7 Return the osso bucco to the sauce and heat gently. Serve with soft semolina or polenta and the broccoli gremolata.

12 FRENCH-TRIMMED LAMB CUTLETS

1 CUP (70G) FRESH BREADCRUMBS

¼ CUP (7G) FINELY CHOPPED FRESH FLAT-LEAF
   PARSLEY

1 TABLESPOON FINELY GRATED PARMESAN

¼ CUP (35G) PLAIN FLOUR

1 EGG

CANOLA OIL, FOR SHALLOW-FRYING

GRAVY, TO SERVE (OPTIONAL)

SWEET POTATO MASH

4 LARGE SWEET POTATOES, PEELED, CHOPPED

25G BUTTER, CHOPPED

½ CUP (125ML) MILK

PINCH OF HIMALAYAN PINK SALT

2 TABLESPOONS PARMESAN (OPTIONAL)

Grant and I both have special ties to the land. I was born on a farm in Duramana, outside of Bathurst, during drought. I've grown up hearing stories from my parents about their struggles, and many of our family friends are still enduring tough times. Grant spent a lot of time at his family's farm in Ariah Park. He would spend school holidays helping his grandparents and uncle with the sheep and crops. We have hundreds of memories of loved ones scattered across the wide open spaces where we feel at home. However, it is the spirit of the people who live on the land that we cherish most. **CHEZZI DENYER**

crumbed lamb cutlets with sweet potato mash

SERVES 4

1 Using your hand, gently flatten the meat on each cutlet.

2 Combine the breadcrumbs, parsley and grated parmesan on a plate. Put the flour on a separate plate. Whisk the egg in a shallow bowl.

3 Coat a cutlet in flour, shaking off the excess. Dip in the egg, then coat in the breadcrumb mixture and place on a plate. Repeat with the remaining cutlets. Cover with plastic wrap and refrigerate for 20 minutes.

4 Meanwhile, to make the sweet potato mash, cook the sweet potato in a large saucepan of boiling water until soft. Drain, then mash with the butter, milk and salt until creamy. Add the parmesan, if using. Cover to keep warm while you cook the cutlets.

5 Pour enough canola oil into a large frying pan to cover the base of the pan. Place the pan over medium heat. Cook the cutlets, in batches, for 3 minutes on each side for medium, or until cooked to your liking. Place on a plate lined with paper towel.

6 Serve the cutlets on the sweet potato mash, with gravy, if desired.

Farming has got to be one of the toughest jobs out there – you're completely dependent on nature, weather and the quality of the soil, which sadly has been degraded. We need to thank farmers more, and truly value what it takes to grow that apple or potato by being willing to pay more for our food. We need to support our farmers and the environment by buying and eating locally and seasonally, and reducing our waste.

This is one of my signature dishes, served to my family and friends and much loved for its layers of rich flavour. It's also the perfect way to use up any left-over vegetables and help eliminate food waste. **RONNIE KAHN**

spinach dahl

SERVES 2–4

TIP

Feel free to add other vegies that you have in your fridge. This adds extra flavour and is a great way to use them up.

1 CUP (225G) MUNG DAHL OR
    RED LENTILS
2 TABLESPOONS GHEE
PINCH OF ASAFOETIDA
1 TEASPOON MUSTARD SEEDS
2 TEASPOONS GRATED FRESH GINGER
1 TEASPOON CUMIN SEEDS
1 TEASPOON GROUND TURMERIC
½ TEASPOON GROUND BLACK PEPPER
6 CURRY LEAVES
1 GREEN CHILLI (OPTIONAL)
1 BUNCH ENGLISH SPINACH,
    STEMS TRIMMED
JUICE OF 1 LEMON
½ BUNCH FRESH CORIANDER
    LEAVES, CHOPPED
PLAIN YOGHURT AND ROTI OR
    STEAMED RICE, TO SERVE

1   Wash the mung dahl at least three times. Drain and set aside.

2   Heat the ghee in a large saucepan over high heat. Stir in the asafoetida and mustard seeds and cook until the seeds start to pop. Stir in the ginger, cumin seeds, turmeric and pepper.

3   Add the mung dahl and pour in 4½ cups (1.125 litres) water, ensuring the mung dahl is generously covered.

4   Stir in the curry leaves and chilli. Bring to the boil, skimming off any froth that forms on top. Reduce the heat to low and simmer the dahl, stirring occasionally, for 30–35 minutes.

5   Discard the curry leaves and chilli. Stir in the spinach and gently heat. Stir in the lemon juice, season with salt and scatter the coriander over the top. Cover, remove from the heat and set aside for 5 minutes.

6   Serve the dahl with yoghurt and roti or rice.

ERICA & NIC DIBDEN

DAIRY FARMERS, CENTRAL TILBA, NSW

———

A ccording to Erica Dibden of the Mountain Valley Farm in Central Tilba, everything she and husband Nic do simply comes back to food. For the couple who have owned the 200-hectare farm on the NSW South Coast for 20 years, each day is about tending to the 400 Jersey cows that supply an estimated 30,000 litres of milk per week, not to mention planting seeds, harvesting crop and making the most of all of it.

"I just love that whole process of nurturing something and turning it into food," Erica says. "I've always believed you are what you eat, and we want the milk that we produce to be the very best it can be for the good health of everyone who buys it."

The couple own the Real Dairy Company, and specifically chose Jersey cows for a number of reasons. "They produce milk high in butter fat and protein, have a lower environmental impact on the farm, are such beautiful creatures and are delightful to see grazing in the fields," Erica says. The farm's range of produce is sold through their ABC Cheese Factory, including bottled milk, yoghurt, cream and many varieties of cheese, like Persian Fetta, Haloumi, Greek-style fetta and cheddar. The farm also boasts an extensive vegetable garden.

"Sometimes when we sit down for a meal, everything on the table originates from our own farm – the vegetables, meat and dairy. Just knowing that is always such a thrill," she says.

Nic starts each day at 4am milking the cows followed by feeding the animals, while Erica starts at 6am overseeing the pasteurisation of the milk in the factory and getting their retail outlet ready for customers in the day ahead.

So far, the drought has not hit too hard at the Mountain Valley Farm, but Erica admits they know it is only a matter of time. "We are starting to lose our grass and the pinch will come when the feed bill doubles, as there is such a shortage of feed across the country," she says. "It is about being able to cope with the extremes of the weather cycles. We know we will get through this, but it is about trying to plan for the next time and the time after that."

Erica purposely uses the word 'resilient' as she describes how farmers across the country are coping with the worst of the drought. "They just don't give up, and everyone needs to remember that farmers are the backbone of this country," she says. "They are the ones who grow the food and, without them, Australia would not eat. I would ask people everywhere to always be mindful when they sit down to eat of the process that food went through to make it to their plate, and the people involved at each step. And, to be thankful for that as well."

ERICA DIBDEN'S

spinach & fetta pie

¼ CUP (60ML) OLIVE OIL,
PLUS EXTRA FOR GREASING

2 BUNCHES ENGLISH SPINACH,
ROUGHLY CHOPPED

2 RED ONIONS, FINELY CHOPPED

10 BUTTON MUSHROOMS, THINLY SLICED

1 CUP FRESH FLAT-LEAF PARSLEY LEAVES,
FINELY CHOPPED

6 GARLIC CLOVES, CRUSHED

10 EGGS, LIGHTLY BEATEN

400G FETTA, CRUMBLED

½ CUP (125ML) POURING CREAM

½ CUP (50G) GRATED CHEDDAR

SALAD GREENS, TO SERVE

1   Preheat the oven to 180°C. Lightly brush a large ovenproof frying pan with olive oil.

2   Steam the spinach until just wilted. Drain well and place in a large bowl. Mix in the onion, mushrooms, parsley and garlic.

3   Whisk the eggs, fetta, cream and olive oil in a separate bowl. Season with salt and pepper. Add to the spinach and mushroom mixture and quickly mix together.

4   Pour the mixture into the frying pan and sprinkle with the grated cheddar. Cover with a sheet of baking paper.

5   Bake the pie for 30 minutes, then remove the baking paper. Bake for a further 20 minutes, until golden brown. Serve with some simple salad greens.

1 LARGE RED ONION, CHOPPED

4 GARLIC CLOVES

JUICE OF 1 LEMON

⅓ CUP (80ML) OLIVE OIL

2 TABLESPOONS RED WINE VINEGAR

1 TABLESPOON HONEY

1 TABLESPOON DRIED OREGANO

2 TEASPOONS SWEET PAPRIKA

2 TEASPOONS SEA SALT

1 TEASPOON CRACKED BLACK PEPPER

2–2.5KG BONE-IN LAMB SHOULDER,
   EXCESS FAT TRIMMED

LEMON WEDGES, TO SERVE

TZATZIKI

1 LEBANESE CUCUMBER

1 CUP (260G) GREEK-STYLE PLAIN YOGHURT

⅓ CUP (80ML) EXTRA VIRGIN OLIVE OIL

JUICE OF ½ LEMON

1 HANDFUL OF FRESH DILL, CHOPPED

1 TABLESPOON ROUGHLY CHOPPED FLAT-LEAF
   PARSLEY

½ TEASPOON GRATED GARLIC

1 TEASPOON SEA SALT

I grew up in the Chewton Bushlands of central Victoria on 10 acres. We didn't have a farm but we did have chooks and a great vegie garden. Throughout my teen years I spent time at a cattle station in central NSW, helping out with mustering. I learnt the importance of supporting and appreciating the hard work of our farmers, and what they provide us with every single day. **BEAU COOK**

slow-roasted lamb shoulder with tzatziki

SERVES 8

———

TIP

The lamb is marinated in the spice mix overnight to allow the flavours to develop.

1 Put the onion, garlic, lemon juice, olive oil, vinegar, honey, oregano, paprika, salt and pepper in a food processor. Process to a coarse paste.

2 Coat the lamb all over with the spice paste. Seal in an airtight container and refrigerate overnight to allow the flavours to develop.

3 To make the tzatziki, grate the cucumber and squeeze out as much liquid as possible. Place in a bowl and mix in the yoghurt, olive oil, lemon juice, dill, parsley, garlic and salt. Cover and refrigerate overnight.

4 Remove the lamb from the fridge 1 hour before cooking. Preheat the oven to 140°C. Wrap the lamb shoulder in baking paper, then wrap in foil, pressing to seal. Transfer to a heavy-based roasting tin and roast for 4 hours, until the meat is tender and falling off the bone.

5 Remove the lamb from the oven and increase the oven temperature to 220°C. Unwrap the lamb and discard the paper and foil. Return the lamb to the roasting tin. Roast for a further 15 minutes, until the lamb starts to brown and caramelise. Remove from the oven and set aside to rest for 10 minutes.

6 Using two forks, pull off the meat in chunks and roughly shred. Serve the lamb with the tzatziki, lemon wedges and a selection of your favourite sides – I love it with Greek salad and roasted spuds.

I arrived in Castlemaine, Victoria, in 2001 and loved the wineries but wondered where the food producers were. The answer was to start a farmers' market, which turned into a huge success. The market, which operates on the first Sunday of the month, now boasts more than 50 stalls featuring produce grown with passion. It is fascinating to see how the community have welcomed the market and it's a great social gathering for families as well as out-of-towners.

This recipe uses produce you'll find in any true farmers' market. With dollops of goat's cheese added before serving, it makes a sumptuous first course or lunch. **SALLY KAPTEIN**

caramelised fennel salad

SERVES 4

4 SMALL FENNEL BULBS

60G BUTTER, CHOPPED

¼ CUP (60ML) EXTRA VIRGIN OLIVE OIL

1 TEASPOON FENNEL SEEDS

2 TABLESPOONS RAW SUGAR

2 GARLIC CLOVES, CRUSHED

½ CUP (30G) FRESH DILL, CHOPPED

1 TEASPOON GRATED LEMON ZEST

½ CUP (60G) SOFT GOAT'S CHEESE (OPTIONAL)

1 Trim the fennel, reserving the fronds. Cut each bulb lengthways, without cutting all the way through to the base, then cut into 1cm slices.

2 Heat the butter and half the olive oil in a large heavy-based frying pan over high heat. Add the fennel and cook for 2–3 minutes on each side or until light golden brown. Transfer to a plate.

3 Add the fennel seeds and raw sugar to the pan. Season with salt and pepper and cook for 1–2 minutes. Return the fennel slices to the pan and reduce the heat to low. Swirl the pan to coat the fennel in the sugar mixture.

4 Place the fennel in a serving bowl. Add the garlic, dill, lemon zest and remaining oil and toss to combine. Add dollops of goat's cheese, if using, and serve garnished with the reserved fennel fronds.

¾ CUP (200G) GREEK-STYLE YOGHURT

⅓ CUP (80ML) TANDOORI PASTE

3 LARGE GARLIC CLOVES, CRUSHED

2CM PIECE GINGER, PEELED, GRATED

1½ TEASPOONS SALT

2 TEASPOONS GROUND CORIANDER

2 TEASPOONS GROUND CUMIN

1 TEASPOON GARAM MASALA

½ TEASPOON GROUND CHILLI

8 CHICKEN THIGH FILLETS, TRIMMED

WARM NAAN BREAD AND SALAD LEAVES,
   TO SERVE

APPLE AND MINT RAITA

1 LEBANESE CUCUMBER, PEELED,
   HALVED LENGTHWAYS

1 GRANNY SMITH APPLE, PEELED

1 CUP (260G) GREEK-STYLE YOGHURT

2 TABLESPOONS CHOPPED FRESH MINT

I'm a city girl and have lived by the beach all my life, but each year we would visit close family friends at Deepwater on the Northern Tablelands of NSW on a beautiful family property that spanned many generations. The memories of riding horses and motorbikes, feeding the chooks and collecting the eggs to cook are everlasting. The days started before the sun was up and it wasn't uncommon for the owners to still be working deep into the night, seven days a week. **JANELLE BLOOM**

tandoori chicken

SERVES 4

1 Combine the yoghurt, tandoori paste, garlic, grated ginger, salt and spices in a large ceramic dish. Add the chicken thighs and turn to coat. Cover and refrigerate for 2 hours or overnight, if time permits.

2 Preheat the oven to 250°C. Place the well-coated chicken on a lightly greased wire rack inside a roasting tin. Cook for 18–20 minutes, until the chicken is cooked through and slightly charred.

3 Meanwhile, to make the raita, use a teaspoon to scrape out and discard the cucumber seeds. Coarsely grate the cucumber and apple, then squeeze out the excess moisture and transfer to a bowl. Stir in the yoghurt and mint and season with salt and pepper. Cover and chill until required.

4 Serve the tandoori chicken with the apple and mint raita, naan bread and salad leaves.

1 X 2KG FREE-RANGE CHICKEN

1 LEMON

⅓ CUP (80ML) EXTRA VIRGIN OLIVE OIL

SEA SALT, TO TASTE

100ML VERJUICE

1 HANDFUL OF THYME SPRIGS

HAZELNUT AND HERB STUFFING

40G TRADITIONALLY SMOKED BELLY BACON,
    RIND REMOVED

2 CHICKEN LIVERS

¼ CUP (60ML) EXTRA VIRGIN OLIVE OIL

2 BROWN ONIONS, FINELY CHOPPED

1 SMALL HANDFUL OF FRESH THYME LEAVES

1 SMALL HANDFUL OF FRESH ROSEMARY LEAVES

1 CUP (90G) FIRMLY PACKED FRESH
    BREADCRUMBS

¼ CUP (50G) PITTED BOTTLED MORELLO
    CHERRIES

¼ CUP (40G) HAZELNUTS, ROASTED, SKINNED,
    CHOPPED

2 GARLIC CLOVES, FINELY CHOPPED

Farming is something you have to be incredibly attuned to. It was the Barossa that really showed me what it was like to live with the seasons – how to live as a farmer. The real difficulty is finding the fortitude to tackle whatever is thrown at you, to jump over roadblocks and find another way. **MAGGIE BEER**

maggie's perfect roast chicken

SERVES 4

1 Take the chicken out of the fridge 1 hour before cooking. Preheat the oven to 200°C fan-forced.

2 To make the stuffing, heat a non-stick frying pan over high heat. Add the bacon and cook, tossing occasionally, for 1 minute. Transfer to a plate and roughly chop when cooled. Cook the chicken livers in the same frying pan for about 30–45 seconds each side, until lightly browned. Transfer the livers to a plate to rest for 5 minutes. Discard any sinew and cut into small chunks.

3 Wipe out the pan and pour in the oil. Cook the onion over medium heat, stirring occasionally, for 10 minutes, until golden. Add the herbs and cook for 1 minute. Tip the mixture into a bowl. Add the breadcrumbs, cherries, hazelnuts and garlic and mix well. Gently stir in the chopped liver and bacon. Add some extra oil, if necessary, to bind the mixture, then set aside to cool.

4 Squeeze a generous amount of lemon juice into the chicken cavity, then fill it with the cooled stuffing. Rub half the oil and the salt over the chicken. Place a wire rack in a shallow roasting tin. Fold the wing tips under the chicken and put it on the rack, breast-side up. Loosely cover the breast with foil. Roast for 30 minutes.

5 Remove the foil, brush the chicken breast with the remaining oil and drizzle with 2 tablespoons of the verjuice. Add a little water to the pan to prevent burning. Reduce the oven to 180°C. Roast the chicken for 30 minutes, until the juices run clear when a skewer is inserted into the thigh joint.

6 Remove the wire rack and turn the chicken to sit breast-side down. Drizzle with the remaining verjuice. Loosely cover with foil. Set aside for 20 minutes before carving. Serve with some roast vegetables.

500G HALOUMI, CUT INTO 1CM SLICES

EXTRA VIRGIN OLIVE OIL

4 CUPS (180G) BABY ROCKET LEAVES

2½ CUPS (440G) CUBED WATERMELON

4 LEBANESE CUCUMBERS, THINLY SLICED

10–12 BASIL LEAVES, TORN

½ LIME, PLUS LIME WEDGES TO SERVE

SEA SALT, TO TASTE

QUICK-PICKLED SHALLOTS

1 FRENCH SHALLOT, VERY THINLY SLICED

1 TABLESPOON APPLE CIDER VINEGAR

PINCH OF CORIANDER SEEDS

PINCH OF SEA SALT

Watermelon offers a somewhat unusual texture in a salad. It's juicy and continues to emit liquid after being cut, so don't let your melon hang around – assemble and eat the salad immediately. The watermelon quantity is flexible and entirely up to you. **HETTY MCKINNON**

watermelon, haloumi & quick-pickled shallot salad

SERVES 4–6

1 To make the quick-pickled shallots, put the sliced shallot in a small bowl and pour over enough of the apple cider vinegar to just cover them. Stir in the coriander seeds, sea salt and 1 tablespoon water. Set aside to pickle for at least 10 minutes or refrigerate overnight if making the pickle a day ahead.

2 Heat a barbecue, grill or frying pan until hot. Coat the haloumi in a little extra virgin olive and gently cook for 1 minute on each side, until golden. Cover with foil to keep warm.

3 Spread the rocket over a large platter. Scatter with the watermelon, cucumber, basil and pickled shallots.

4 Tear the warm haloumi into pieces and add it to the salad. Squeeze the lime juice over the top and drizzle with some extra virgin olive oil. Season with sea salt and freshly ground black pepper. Serve immediately, with extra lime wedges on the side.

My dad grew up in Bukovyna, Ukraine, and came to Australia as a post-World War II refugee when his family were posted to work on a farm in Crookwell. His love of the land eventually saw him realise his dream of buying a sheep farm in Inverell. When it was just the two of us staying on the farm, he had a rule that we were only to cook something from the land. As sheep were so valuable, this often meant eating what roamed wild on the farm, such as kangaroo, rabbit, pig or the odd duck. This recipe was one of our favourites, blending my dad's Ukrainian Carpathian heritage with an Australian twist. **SONJA BERNYK**

kangaroo goulash

SERVES 4

1KG DICED KANGAROO LEG MEAT

2 TABLESPOONS PLAIN FLOUR

¼ CUP (60ML) OLIVE OIL

1 RED ONION, FINELY CHOPPED

2 CARROTS, FINELY CHOPPED

1 RED CAPSICUM, THINLY SLICED

3 GARLIC CLOVES, FINELY CHOPPED

2 TABLESPOONS TOMATO PASTE

2 TABLESPOONS SWEET PAPRIKA

4 ROMA TOMATOES, CHOPPED

1¼ CUPS (310ML) CHICKEN STOCK

½ TEASPOON DRIED ROSEMARY

1 BAY LEAF

1 TABLESPOON FINELY CHOPPED FRESH DILL

MASHED POTATO, SOUR CREAM AND
    PICKLED DILL CUCUMBERS, TO SERVE

1   Put the kangaroo meat in a large bowl. Sprinkle with the flour and toss to coat.

2   Heat 2 tablespoons of the oil in a large heavy-based saucepan over medium–high heat. Cook the kangaroo meat in three batches, until well browned on all sides. Transfer to a bowl.

3   Reduce the heat to medium and add the rest of the oil to the pan. Add the onion and carrot and cook, stirring occasionally, for 5 minutes. Add the capsicum and garlic and cook, stirring occasionally, for 5 minutes. Stir in the tomato paste and paprika and cook for 30 seconds. Add the tomato and cook, stirring occasionally, for 5 minutes, until softened.

4   Return the kangaroo meat and any juices to the pan. Stir in the stock, rosemary and bay leaf. Cover and bring to a simmer. Reduce the heat to low and simmer, stirring occasionally, for 1½–2 hours, until the meat is tender.

5   Season with salt and pepper and sprinkle with the dill. Serve the goulash with mashed potato, sour cream and dill cucumbers.

I was born and bred into farming and loved having the opportunity to raise my own family in such a great location. I love the prep work of ploughing and the satisfaction of seeing our potatoes get great reviews from our customers. But the best thing about being a farmer is being your own boss. Australian farmers are undervalued. It's imperative that people – especially children who live in cities – are educated about agriculture and its importance as nowadays there is a disconnection between city and country. **WAYNE ADAMS**

cheesy potato bake

SERVES 4

4 NICOLA POTATOES, THINLY SLICED

1 BROWN ONION, DICED

300G BACON, DICED

300G CREAM CHEESE, DICED

3 CUPS (300G) GRATED TASTY CHEESE

1 Preheat the oven to 200°C. Layer the potato, onion, bacon, cream cheese and tasty cheese in a greased 6-cup (1.5-litre) ovenproof dish, reserving 1 cup of the grated tasty cheese.

2 Scatter the reserved grated cheese over the top of the potato mixture. Cover and bake for 20 minutes, then uncover and bake for 25–30 minutes, until the potato is soft and the top is golden brown.

1 TABLESPOON VEGETABLE OIL

1 LEEK, TRIMMED, HALVED LENGTHWAYS,
   THINLY SLICED

400G ZUCCHINI, DICED

1 LONG GREEN CHILLI, DESEEDED,
   SLICED, PLUS EXTRA TO SERVE

2 GARLIC CLOVES, FINELY CHOPPED

4½ CUPS (1.125 LITRES) VEGETABLE STOCK

120G TRIMMED, TORN KALE LEAVES
   (ABOUT ½ BUNCH)

400G CAN CANNELLINI BEANS,
   RINSED, DRAINED

250G TRIMMED ENGLISH SPINACH
   LEAVES (ABOUT 2 BUNCHES)

TOASTED MIXED SEEDS AND
   CRUMBLED FETTA, TO SERVE

I just love creating and styling recipes using farm-fresh Aussie fruit and vegies, pork, chicken, lamb and beef, plus eggs and dairy. A few years ago, after a shattering drought, I spent time on a vast lamb farm just outside of Hay in NSW. It was especially during this time that I realised how tough farming is in Australia. I so appreciate and value our dedicated, hard-working and passionate farmers and growers. **ANNETTE FORREST**

green vegie & cannellini bean soup

SERVES 4

1   Heat the oil in a large saucepan over medium heat. Add the leek and cook, stirring often, for 4–5 minutes, until softened. Add the zucchini, chilli and garlic and cook, stirring occasionally, for 5 minutes.

2   Pour in the stock. Partially cover the pan and bring to the boil. Add the kale and cannellini beans. Cook over medium–high heat, stirring often, until the kale wilts. Reduce the heat to a simmer and cook, uncovered, for 5 minutes, until the zucchini is tender.

3   Stir in the spinach and cook, stirring, until just wilted. Set the soup aside to cool for 5 minutes.

4   Using a stick blender, blend the soup until smooth. Return to the heat and gently reheat over low heat.

5   Ladle the soup into bowls. Scatter the toasted mixed seeds and fetta over the top to serve.

Farming life has really become personal since I purchased a farm property in the Southern Highlands earlier this year. I have friends who also have farms in the area and I love that I'm now able to have my own chickens. I'm considering getting some goats and my own horse – something I have long dreamed of being able to do. **MICHELLE BRIDGES**

chorizo-stuffed sweet potatoes

SERVES 4

————————

Recipe from *Food for Life* by Michelle Bridges, published by Pan Macmillan Australia.

4 X 250G SWEET POTATOES, SCRUBBED

1 CURED CHORIZO (ABOUT 125G), FINELY CHOPPED

1 BUNCH SILVERBEET, STEMS REMOVED, LEAVES FINELY SHREDDED

1 CORN COB, KERNELS REMOVED

¼ CUP (25G) FINELY GRATED TASTY CHEESE

1 Preheat the oven to 200°C. Put the sweet potatoes on a baking tray and bake for 45 minutes, until tender when tested with a skewer in the centre.

2 Meanwhile, cook the chopped chorizo in a large non-stick frying pan over medium–low heat, stirring occasionally, for 12 minutes, until the oil releases and the chorizo is golden. Add the shredded silverbeet and cook, stirring, for 3 minutes, until wilted. Add the corn and stir until well combined. Remove from the heat, cover and stand for 2 minutes. Season to taste.

3 Split the sweet potatoes lengthways, without cutting them all the way through. Sprinkle with the grated cheese, then fill with the chorizo mixture.

PAUL DAWSON

PAWSUP COORDINATOR, ARMIDALE, NSW

————

P aul Dawson has ventured into city life and spent time overseas, but time and time again he feels the inevitable pull back to the land. "My family have spent their life on the land – it's kind of in my blood," he says. "Growing up, I was always outdoors helping on the family farm and never too far away from a horse or a dog."

With his boots firmly back on the red soil, these days Paul is based in Armidale, NSW, where he is the Program Coordinator at PawsUp, an innovative initiative run by not-for-profit youth organisation BackTrack. The program pairs at-risk teen boys with a working dog and gives them responsibility for training and caring for their four-legged friend, offering an opportunity to build trust, establish relationships and re-engage with the community.

"The dogs are always there, which is something that we all need," says Paul. "The dogs are clever, they don't judge, and they live in the moment."

The PawsUp team use mainly border collies and kelpies, both of which, in addition to being stellar working dogs, make perfect companions for the boys thanks to their resilient, easy-to-train natures and a real willingness to please. Paul's job is to oversee the program and make sure the young people in his care are feeling safe, comfortable and prepared to learn. The dogs offer a strong sense of safety and comfort to the boys, also boosting their self-confidence and providing life-long lessons in self-discipline. "It's really special watching a young person with a dog from the day they first meet and then on their journey to get back on track," he says.

Since its inception a decade ago, launched by former Gunnedah youth worker Bernie Shakeshaft, PawsUp has worked with more than 1000 youths. In that time, Armidale has seen its local crime rate drop by 50%. The initiative works in conjunction with BackTrack's BT Works program, an employment-focused social enterprise that mentors and trains young people in skills such as fencing for local farmers, eventually supporting them to transition into paid work.

"I really enjoy witnessing their stages of change and growth," says Paul of working with the boys. "One boy who came through BackTrack was homeless, sleeping in the back of a car, stealing for food. He is now working in our BT Works crew with a beautiful little family. Obviously there are still struggles in life, but he is in a good spot and I'm really proud of him."

The 2018 cinematic release of *BackTrack Boys*, a documentary following a trio of teens involved in the PawsUp program, has piqued the nation's interest in the work carried out by Paul and his colleagues, such that he now spends time on the road mentoring other communities to adopt a BackTrack-style youth program in their region.

Like most in rural Australia, BackTrack has been touched by the drought. "Some of the farmers we rely on for work are a bit short on resources," Paul explains. "The drought has been an emotional journey for many in our community." The PawsUp program offers a welcome boost for a community Paul describes as "hardworking, down-to-earth legends".

"It's bloody nice when you see a kid that can't look you in the eye suddenly start joining in the conversation and smiling – that's pretty special."

PAUL DAWSON'S

best-ever cheese toastie

SERVES 1
_____

EXTRA VIRGIN OLIVE OIL, FOR FRYING

LOADS OF BUTTER

2 THICK SLICES WHITE BREAD

A GENEROUS HANDFUL OF GRATED
    VINTAGE CHEDDAR

A GENEROUS HANDFUL OF GRATED
    MOZZARELLA, GOUDA OR GRUYERE

SEA SALT, TO TASTE

TOMATO RELISH, TO SERVE

1   Heat the oil in a cast-iron frying pan over
    medium heat (you don't want it too hot or
    the toast will burn).

2   Generously butter each slice of bread. Lay
    the bread on a board, buttered side down,
    and top one slice with the cheeses. Season
    with sea salt and freshly ground black pepper.
    Top with the other slice of bread.

3   Add the sandwich to the pan and weigh it
    down with a plate and something heavy to
    hold it in place. Cook for 3–4 minutes, until
    the toast is golden brown. Turn and cook the
    other side until golden brown and the cheese
    is melted and oozing.

4   It's tempting to eat the toastie as soon as it
    comes out of the pan, but be careful not to
    burn your mouth. Sprinkle with extra salt
    and pepper and serve with tomato relish.

20G BUTTER, SOFTENED, PLUS EXTRA
TO MAKE GRAVY (OPTIONAL)

2 GREEN ONIONS, FINELY CHOPPED

2 GARLIC CLOVES, FINELY CHOPPED

1 x 1.8KG CHICKEN (PREFERABLY WITH GIBLETS)

1 TABLESPOON OLIVE OIL

200G BACON, TRIMMED, CHOPPED

250G SMALL PICKLING ONIONS, PEELED

500G SMALL WHITE POTATOES, SCRUBBED

6 CARROTS, PEELED

325ML HOT NERADA BLACK TEA, STRAINED

A FEW BAY LEAVES

1 SPRIG THYME

3 LEEKS, TRIMMED, CUT INTO 10CM LENGTHS

2–3 TEASPOONS PLAIN FLOUR (OPTIONAL)

It's tough making a quality Australian product in a global economy. For us, if our business is to be sustainable into the future, we need to ensure we keep our client base in Australia. If we want to keep our farmers, we need to support them and buy locally. **TONY POYNER**

chicken & leek with tea

SERVES 4

1   Combine the butter, green onion and garlic in a bowl. Season with salt and pepper. Pat the chicken dry and rub the butter mixture inside the cavity. Tie the legs together and tuck the wings under. Preheat the oven to 200°C.

2   Heat the oil in a flameproof casserole dish over medium–high heat. Add the bacon and cook, stirring occasionally, for 5 minutes, until crisp. Transfer to a plate. Add the giblets, if using, to the dish and cook, stirring occasionally, for 4 minutes, until brown. Set aside on a separate plate. Add the chicken to the dish and cook, turning, for 3 minutes, until browned all over, then transfer to a large bowl. Add the pickling onions to the dish and cook for 3 minutes, until glazed. Transfer to a separate bowl. Add the potatoes and carrots to the dish, adding more oil if necessary. Cook for 5 minutes, until browned. Transfer to a separate bowl.

3   Return the chicken to the dish, breast-side up. Place the giblets, potatoes and carrots around the chicken. Pour in the hot tea, add the herbs and season with salt and pepper. Arrange the leeks around the chicken. Cover and bake for 30 minutes, turning the chicken and vegetables twice, being careful not to break up the leeks. Add the pickling onions and bacon. Bake for a further 45 minutes, until the chicken is cooked and the juices run clear.

4   Place the chicken on a heated dish with the vegetables and cover to keep warm. If desired, make a gravy by reducing the pan juices over low heat. Season, then stir in the flour and extra butter to thicken the gravy. Serve the gravy with the chicken and vegetables.

My father came from a long line of farmers, and farming has always been in his blood. In his early days, he had a large sheep and wheat farm at Yeelanna, a small town 80km north of Port Lincoln. Towards the end of World War II, the Australian Government initiated a scheme that saw roughly 14,000 Italian Prisoners of War (POWs) brought out to replace the men who had been pulled from farms to fight overseas. My father was allocated a number of POWs, who were immediately put to work harvesting and bagging up the wheat. Everyone pitched in at harvesting time, and my mother helped by sewing up the bags of wheat. Homesick and yearning for some Italian food, the POWs proceeded to teach her how to make spaghetti bolognese. **JANET MITCHELL**

POW's spaghetti bolognese

SERVES 4

———————

2 TABLESPOONS OLIVE OIL

1 BROWN ONION, FINELY CHOPPED

4 GARLIC CLOVES, SLICED

1 SMALL CARROT, CHOPPED

1 STALK CELERY, CHOPPED

100G BACON, CHOPPED

PINCH OF SALT

800G LAMB MINCE

400ML RED WINE

600G CANNED WHOLE ITALIAN
  TOMATOES, ROUGHLY CHOPPED

3 TABLESPOONS CHOPPED MIXED
  FRESH HERBS, SUCH AS THYME,
  FLAT-LEAF PARSLEY AND ROSEMARY

400G SPAGHETTI

GRATED PARMESAN, TO SERVE

1 Heat the olive oil in a large frying pan over medium-high heat. Add the onion, garlic, carrot, celery, bacon and salt. Cook, stirring occasionally, for 15 minutes, until the vegetables are caramelised.

2 Add the lamb mince and cook, breaking up the lumps, for 6–8 minutes, until browned. Pour in the wine and bring to the boil, then reduce the heat and simmer until reduced by half. Add the canned tomato and simmer for 30 minutes. Add the fresh herbs and cook for 10 minutes. Season to taste.

3 While the sauce is cooking, cook the spaghetti in plenty of boiling salted water until al dente. Drain, then divide the pasta among four bowls. Top with the sauce and sprinkle with grated parmesan and freshly ground black pepper.

AMBER WINZER & JASON WRIGHT

DROVERS, REGIONAL VIC AND NSW

Amber Winzer and Jason Wright's son William was only four weeks old when they bundled up the baby blankets and took him droving. "We were contracting right up until I was 37 weeks pregnant," Amber explains. "I was getting over a caesarean when Jason said we were heading out on the road again and asked if I was ready. I said, 'Well, I guess I'd better be!' and off we went."

As partners in Burrabogie Livestock and Contracting, Amber, 40, and Jason, 48, organise their lives around the needs of other farmers. Whether they are droving cattle along travelling stock reserves or mustering wily rangeland goats, it's relentless work driven by real passion.

"We live and breathe it 24/7," Jason says. "Looking after the cattle is our responsibility. You can't just say I don't want to get out of bed this morning; you've got to get up and find them water and grass. After a couple of months the cattle start to trust that you'll take care of them... Keeping them healthy is what it's all about."

Amber, an equine nurse who grew up on a cattle property in north-eastern Victoria, and Jason, the son of a Queensland pineapple farmer, know the highs and lows of farming all too well. In 2016 Jason sold his share of a large cattle trading business in Rutherglen, Victoria, when cattle prices were at an all-time high; two years later they found themselves in drought droving 1300 cattle in a loop around the Riverina for five months, often trucking in 100,000 litres of water a day just to keep them alive.

"It's probably one of the toughest jobs I've had to do," Jason admits. "The cattle were in pretty poor condition when we got them and sometimes we'd turn up for water and the windmills wouldn't be pumping. But by the time they went home they were very healthy. That's what we pride ourselves in, how we look after the stock."

Jason's worn out plenty of swags but the couple now opt for a 48-foot semi-trailer (complete with king-size bed) and travel with six stockhorses and up to 15 working dogs. Their day begins before sunrise when they set up traffic warning signs before packing up camp and taking down the electric tape that corrals the herd overnight. Throughout the day they are on constant alert for broken fences and straying stock as they push the mob 5 to 10 kilometres before bunkering back down for the night.

But despite the challenges of a nomadic life, life off the land is unimaginable. "Droving is certainly not the romantic novel Jason described," Amber laughs. "But I love it all, even the bad days are good days. It's a passion that runs in your blood. At the end of the day the sunsets out on the wide-open spaces of the Hay plains are just spectacular. Of an afternoon we love to sit on the riverbank and enjoy a beer. It's just a beautiful way of life."

1 PIECE SILVERSIDE (APPROXIMATELY 1KG)

½ CUP (110G) FIRMLY PACKED BROWN SUGAR

1 CUP (250ML) MALT VINEGAR

4 CLOVES

1 BAY LEAF

ROASTED OR STEAMED CARROTS AND
    BRUSSELS SPROUTS, TO SERVE

MALT VINEGAR, TO SERVE

CREAMY MASH

700G DIRTY POTATOES, WASHED, PEELED,
    CUT INTO QUARTERS

50G BUTTER

1 CUP (250ML) CREAM OR MILK

½ CUP (45G) GRATED PARMESAN

MUSTARD SAUCE

½ CUP (125G) WHOLEGRAIN HONEY MUSTARD

60G BUTTER, CHOPPED

¼ CUP (60G) FIRMLY PACKED BROWN SUGAR

300ML THICK CREAM

AMBER WINZER'S

silverside

SERVES 4

1 Put the silverside, brown sugar, vinegar, cloves and bay leaf in a large saucepan over medium heat. Pour in enough cold water to cover the silverside. Cover and bring to a simmer, then reduce the heat to low. Simmer for 1½ hours, until tender. Replenish the water during cooking if necessary.

2 Transfer the silverside to a plate, cover and set aside to rest for 10 minutes before slicing.

3 Meanwhile, to make the mash, boil the potatoes until soft. Drain well, then return to the pan. Add the butter, cream and parmesan and mash well until smooth. Season with salt and pepper and keep warm.

4 To make the mustard sauce, combine the mustard, butter, brown sugar and cream in a saucepan over medium–high heat. Bring to the boil, then reduce the heat and simmer for 5 minutes, until slightly thickened.

5 Serve the sliced silverside with the creamy mash and the mustard sauce, alongside the carrots and brussels sprouts with a splash of malt vinegar.

BORDER COLLIE
WORKING DOGS

"Hey, I'm Sophie. I'm a short-haired border collie. My mates would probably describe me as the leader of the pack. Us border collies are a pretty good-natured lot, and we pride ourselves on being some of the most faithful, courageous, kind-hearted dogs around. Because we're so intelligent, we're very trainable, which suits my owners, Amber and Jason, just fine. We live a nomadic life, travelling from place to place helping farmers throughout the whole of eastern Australia.

My job is to help herd the cattle, moving them on to greener pastures. I help to look after the cows and keep an eye out for any rogue operators who are straying from the herd. Border collies are top working dogs, because we're very smart (if I may say so myself). We're the philosophers of the dog world – we think situations through, and we've got initiative – so our owners don't need to micromanage us, which makes their job easier.

I work with 15 other 'cow dogs', as Jason calls us. Lots of my mates here are kelpies, and the rest of us are Jason's own breed of cow dog, with the majority of our make-up being border collie. (Just between us, I know I'm Jason's favourite, but let's not tell the others that). Jason and Amber breed us working dogs and raise us from pups, so we're all pretty close. When you live and work together every day, your relationship with your human is everything, so it helps that we get on pretty well.

A typical day begins when the stars are still twinkling overhead and the birds are yet to start their morning racket. Jason is the first in the camp to rise. He lets us off the chain and we take off to have a run around the paddock. Then I head out with three or four other dogs to work the cows for a couple of hours, before I come off the paddock for a sniff about and a snooze in the sun.

We recently had a new arrival in our camp, Jason and Amber's baby boy, William. Once I've knocked off for the day, you'll often find me with my head in the pram, giving William's toes a lick and keeping him up to date with what happened out in the paddock. After that, it's dinner time. Us working dogs are professional athletes, so we need our humans to keep us well fed and watered so we can perform at our best on the job. My favourite thing to chow down on after a long day moving the cattle is a tasty dog biscuit (they're better than they sound, trust me). Jason often cooks a steak for the humans' dinner, and if we're lucky he'll throw us some.

All in all, I'm a pretty happy camper living out here on the land. My favourite part of my job, aside from getting to spend 24/7 running about with my doggo mates, is looking after the cows, making sure they find some feed and water, and lending a helping paw to the farmers. As Jason says, us dogs can do the work of several men for a fraction of the price (and we're more reliable), so we've been invaluable during the drought. I work seven days a week, so there are no lazy Sundays on the couch chewing a bone for me, but I wouldn't have it any other way."

⅓ CUP (80ML) EXTRA VIRGIN OLIVE OIL,
   PLUS EXTRA TO SERVE
2 BROWN ONIONS, DICED
2 GARLIC CLOVES, CRUSHED
2 LARGE CARROTS, DICED
2 STALKS CELERY, DICED
2 DRIED BAY LEAVES
1 SMOKED HAM HOCK
2¼ CUPS (500G) GREEN SPLIT PEAS, RINSED
2 CHICKEN STOCK CUBES

200G CRÈME FRAÎCHE
1 TABLESPOON DIJON MUSTARD
1 BUNCH CHIVES, SNIPPED
SEA SALT, TO TASTE
1 BUNCH FRESH FLAT-LEAF PARSLEY,
   ROUGHLY CHOPPED
500G FROZEN BABY PEAS
FRESH CRUSTY BREAD WITH LOADS
   OF BUTTER, TO SERVE

The smell of pea and ham soup on winter days brings back fond memories from my childhood, sitting at the big table in the kitchen of our family farmhouse, with the soup bubbling away on the wood stove. To this day it is one of my favourite soups. I make it the same way my mum did, but I've added the bright green freshness at the end with some frozen peas, parsley and a rich garnish of crème fraîche, mustard and chives. This is a great soup to serve a crowd, and it's even more delicious reheated the day after it's cooked. If it's too thick, add some water. **JANE GRYLLS**

pea & ham soup

SERVES 4

1 Heat the olive oil in a large heavy-based saucepan over medium heat. Add the onion, garlic, carrot and celery and cook, stirring occasionally, for 10 minutes, until the onion is transparent.

2 Add the bay leaves, ham hock, split peas, chicken stock cubes and 4 litres water. Bring to the boil, skimming the foam that rises to the surface. Reduce the heat and simmer, stirring occasionally, for 2½–3 hours, until the split peas have completely broken down and the ham is falling off the bone.

3 While the soup is cooking, add the crème fraîche to a small bowl and stir in the mustard and snipped chives. Chill until ready to serve.

4 Remove the bay leaves and ham hock from the soup. Take all the meat from the bones and skin. Shred the meat and return it to the soup. Season to taste with sea salt and black pepper.

5 When ready to serve, bring the soup to the boil, add the parsley and frozen peas and cook for 5 minutes.

6 Ladle the soup into bowls and serve with a spoonful of the crème fraîche. Drizzle with extra virgin olive oil and serve with some fresh crusty bread with butter.

100G DICED SPECK

50G UNSALTED BUTTER

2 WHITE ONIONS, THINLY SLICED

1 BUNCH SILVERBEET, STEMS THINLY SLICED,
  LEAVES TORN INTO SMALL PIECES

3 EGGS

200G SOUR CREAM

½ CUP (50G) GRATED GRUYERE

100G GOAT'S FETTA, CRUMBLED

GROUND WHITE PEPPER, TO TASTE

SWEET PAPRIKA, TO TASTE

FINELY SHREDDED ROCKET, LEMON JUICE
  AND OLIVE OIL, TO SERVE

PASTRY

3⅔ CUPS (550G) PLAIN FLOUR

1 TEASPOON SALT

300G CHILLED UNSALTED BUTTER, DICED

1 EGG

½ CUP (125G) SOUR CREAM

Since moving to the NSW Hawkesbury region six years ago, direct from Kings Cross, I have forged many friendships with local farmers. I now not only promote the bountiful produce from the Hawkesbury, but also deliver a range of produce to the city each week. **MARTIN BOETZ**

onion, silverbeet & gruyere tart

SERVES 8–10

1 To make the pastry, combine the flour and salt in a food processor. With the motor running, add the butter, one piece at a time, and process until well combined. Add the egg and sour cream and pulse until it just forms a ball.

2 Turn the pastry out onto a lightly floured surface. Roll out until 3mm thick. Transfer to a deep 30cm loose-based tart tin and trim any excess pastry. Place in the fridge for 20 minutes. Preheat the oven to 200°C.

3 To make the filling, cook the speck in a large frying pan over medium heat, stirring often, until the fat starts to render. Add the butter, onion and silverbeet stems and gently cook, stirring, for 10–12 minutes, until soft. Add the silverbeet leaves. Cook, stirring, for 5 minutes, until wilted. Transfer to a colander to cool and drain.

4 Place the tart tin on a baking tray and prick the pastry base all over with a fork. Line the pastry with baking paper and fill with baking weights or dried beans. Bake the tart for 20 minutes, then remove the weights and paper and bake for a further 10 minutes, until the pastry base looks dry.

5 Whisk the eggs, sour cream and cheeses in a bowl. Fold in the cooled silverbeet mixture. Generously season with salt, white pepper and sweet paprika.

6 Reduce the oven to 180°C. Spoon the filling into the pastry case. Bake for 30–40 minutes, until the pastry is crisp and cooked through and the filling is just set. Cool the tart in the tin a little before slicing, then serve topped with shredded rocket, dressed with some lemon juice and olive oil.

1.8–2KG LEG OF LAMB, FRENCHED
   (ASK YOUR BUTCHER TO DO THIS)
4 ANCHOVY FILLETS, DRIED ON PAPER
   TOWEL, EACH CUT INTO 3 PIECES
3 LARGE GARLIC CLOVES, QUARTERED
1 TABLESPOON EXTRA VIRGIN OLIVE OIL
200G PIECE PORK RIND WITH 5MM OF
   FAT ATTACHED

2 BOUQUET GARNIS (INCLUDING THYME
   SPRIGS, A FRESH BAY LEAF AND A SMALL
   PIECE OF CELERY)
1 CUP (250ML) FULL-FLAVOURED VEAL STOCK
   (OR CHICKEN STOCK OR LAMB STOCK)
1 CUP (250ML) DRY WHITE WINE

My only connection with the land dates from when I was about nine until I left home to attend university nine years after that. My grandfather lived with the family and he and my mother made quite a team in the vegetable garden and the duck yard, and my father was responsible for the milking of the cow and the separation of the milk. It was not a large property and farming was certainly not the main income producer. My parents planned and created a holiday camp, but until it was well-established we lived on a lot of eggs, milk and potatoes, and modest purchases from the local shops and butcher. My father also went fishing and we enjoyed plenty of flathead. **STEPHANIE ALEXANDER**

7-hour leg of lamb with anchovy & garlic

SERVES 6

1 Preheat the oven to 120°C.
2 With the tip of a sharp knife, make six deep incisions into each side of the lamb. Insert a piece of anchovy and garlic into each incision. Season the lamb with salt and pepper. Heat the oil in a large heavy-based frying pan over medium heat. Cook the lamb on all sides until a rich golden brown.
3 Put the pork rind, fat-side down, in an enamelled cast-iron casserole dish that will hold the lamb snugly and has a tight-fitting lid. Add the bouquet garnis and lamb, then pour in the stock and wine and put on the lid. (If you are at all unsure of the lid's tight fit, mix some flour and water to a paste and smear it around the edges to seal where the lid fits onto the pot.) Stand the dish on a baking tray and transfer to the oven. Forget about it for 7 hours.

4 When ready to serve, remove the dish from the oven and carefully transfer the meat to a hot serving dish. Pour the juices into a jug, leave to settle for 5 minutes, then spoon off most of the fat that has risen to the top. Transfer the juices to a wide frying pan and boil rapidly over high heat until reduced by about one-third.
5 Gently carve the lamb (it will be very tender and will break up). Cut the pork rind into small slivers. Moisten the sliced lamb with the cooking juices and serve with mashed potato.

I've spent wonderful times in Jen's warm farmhouse kitchens in South Australia and western Victoria, havens where the promise of tea and the beautifully thought-out next meal is never far away. And then there are her recipes. Back when a 'hack' was what you gave the city slicker to ride, she was working on innovative ways to make everything from Claudia Roden's orange cake to the classic schnitzel shorter, simpler and easier without compromising on taste. You might see it as another example of Aussie farming ingenuity but, as I see it, it's more proof of the smarts of one of the best cooks I know. Jen's moment of genius here is to dunk the chunks of chicken thighs in melted butter so you get the buttery flavour without the frying pan... and by using the oven, you can make more golden schnitzelly goodness than any frying pan can ever handle. Genius! **MATT PRESTON**

jen's chicken nuggets

SERVES 4

Recipe from *Cook Book* by Matt Preston, published by Plum.

12 (1.5KG) CHICKEN THIGH FILLETS

100G BUTTER, MELTED

2 CUPS (120G) PANKO BREADCRUMBS

SEA SALT, TO TASTE

2 BABY COS OR GEM LETTUCES,
   LEAVES SEPARATED

½ CUP (120G) AIOLI OR MAYONNAISE

½ CUP (125ML) SWEET CHILLI SAUCE
   OR MANGO CHUTNEY

1 LEMON, CUT INTO WEDGES

1 BUNCH CORIANDER, LEAVES PICKED,
   STEMS THINLY SLICED

1 Preheat the oven to 220°C. Line two large baking trays with baking paper.

2 Use a mallet or rolling pin to flatten the chicken thigh fillets between two sheets of baking paper until they are an even thickness. Cut the chicken into 3cm pieces.

3 Dunk the chicken into the melted butter, a few pieces at a time. Toss in the breadcrumbs to coat, then arrange on the trays, leaving room between each piece.

4 Bake the nuggets for 15–20 minutes, turning halfway, until golden and cooked through. Sprinkle with sea salt.

5 Serve the nuggets in lettuce cups, with some aioli or mayonnaise, some sweet chilli sauce or mango chutney, as well as a squeeze of lemon and fresh coriander.

Having grown up in my parents' pub in the English countryside, with local farms and the surrounding land as my playground, I've always felt the precious connection between the produce we see being grown in the fields and the food that ends up on our plates.

This is a fun little dish I had when I was a younger kid – it's a bit of a play on chilli, with a delicious vibrancy. I serve it with a charred chilli per person. Depending on how spicy you like your food, feel free to chop and stir in just a little, or the whole thing if you think you can handle it! **JAMIE OLIVER**

chilli con carne meatballs

SERVES 4

1¾ CUPS (350G) BROWN BASMATI RICE

4 GREEN CHILLIES

OLIVE OIL, FOR FRYING

3 GREEN ONIONS, THINLY SLICED

1 RED CAPSICUM, CHOPPED

4 SPRIGS CORIANDER, LEAVES AND STEMS
    CHOPPED SEPARATELY

2 X 400G CANS WHOLE ITALIAN TOMATOES

2 X 400G CANS BLACK BEANS, RINSED,
    DRAINED

500G LEAN BEEF MINCE

1 TEASPOON SMOKED PAPRIKA

½ TEASPOON GROUND CHILLI

½ CUP (130G) GREEK-STYLE PLAIN YOGHURT

1 LIME, CUT INTO WEDGES

1 Cook the rice in a saucepan of boiling salted water over medium heat for 25 minutes, until soft. Drain well, cover with a lid and set aside.

2 Preheat a grill to high. Prick the chillies and place them under the grill, turning often, for 10 minutes, until blackened.

3 Meanwhile, heat some olive oil in a large deep frying pan over medium heat. Cook the green onion, capsicum and coriander stems for 5 minutes, until softened. Pour in the canned tomatoes and 200ml water, breaking up the tomatoes with a spoon. Bring to the boil and add the black beans.

4 While the sauce is cooking, place the beef into a mixing bowl, add the spices and a good pinch of salt and pepper and mix well. Using wet hands, roll tablespoons of the mixture into balls. Add the meatballs to the sauce and cook for 6–8 minutes, until the sauce is thick and the meatballs are cooked through.

5 Fold the chopped coriander leaves through the rice. Divide among four serving plates and top with the meatballs and sauce, the blackened chillies, yoghurt and lime wedges for squeezing.

Our property, JS Grazing, is a family-operated beef cattle enterprise at Injune in Queensland. Along with our two young sons, Henry and Leo, we run a commercial Angus herd. Jeremy recently took the reins of the family business but his parents, Jeffrey and Jennifer, are still involved.

Our boys are becoming more involved in the day-to-day running of our properties and although we feel it's imperative to give them a broad education, we hope that they will return to the land some day. It is important to us as primary producers that our children understand where their food comes from and we try to involve them in both the paddock side of our business as well as food preparation. They are both keen cooks and love helping at mealtimes, particularly with this favourite sausage roll recipe. **JULIE AND JEREMY SHAW**

tucker box sausage rolls

MAKES 24

500G BEEF MINCE

1 ZUCCHINI, GRATED

1 CARROT, GRATED

1 BROWN ONION, FINELY CHOPPED

1 TABLESPOON CRUSHED GARLIC

1 EGG

½ PACKET FRENCH ONION SOUP MIX

1 CUP (110G) PACKAGED BREADCRUMBS

2 TABLESPOONS SNIPPED FRESH CHIVES

4 SHEETS READY-ROLLED FROZEN
   PUFF PASTRY, THAWED

MILK, FOR BRUSHING

2 TABLESPOONS POPPY SEEDS

TOMATO SAUCE, TO SERVE

1 Preheat the oven to 200°C. Line a large baking tray with baking paper.

2 Combine the beef, zucchini, carrot, onion, garlic, egg, soup mix, breadcrumbs and chives in a bowl. Season with salt and pepper. Mix until the mixture has a paste-like consistency.

3 Cut the pastry sheets in half. Spoon a line of the beef mixture along one long edge of each pastry piece. Roll the pastry over to enclose the filling. Cut each roll into three sausage rolls. Place onto the tray.

4 Brush the sausage rolls with milk. Sprinkle with the poppy seeds. Bake for 25–30 minutes, until golden brown. Serve with tomato sauce.

8 CUPS (2 LITRES) VEGETABLE BROTH

2 TABLESPOONS OLIVE OIL

80G BUTTER

2 BROWN ONIONS, FINELY CHOPPED

2 GARLIC CLOVES, CRUSHED

400G MEDIUM-GRAIN BROWN RICE,
SOAKED OVERNIGHT IN WATER

200G ZUCCHINI, FINELY CHOPPED

2 BUNCHES ASPARAGUS, FINELY CHOPPED

1¼ CUPS (125G) FINELY GRATED PARMESAN

JUICE OF ½ LEMON

THINLY SLICED GREEN ONION AND
MINT LEAVES, TO SERVE

The rice needs to be soaked for as long as possible before cooking. A few hours out on the bench is okay, but if you can leave it overnight, it will start to ferment a little, which helps with nutrition and flavour. To speed up the fermentation, you can add a spoonful of natural yoghurt or some whey to the soaking liquid. **MATT STONE**

brown rice, asparagus & zucchini risotto

SERVES 6

1 Pour the broth into a saucepan. Bring to the boil over medium–high heat, then reduce to a low simmer.

2 Heat a large heavy-based saucepan over medium heat. Add the oil, half the butter and the onion. Cook, stirring often, for 10 minutes. Stir in the crushed garlic and cook for 2 minutes.

3 Drain the rice and add it to the onion mixture. Cook, stirring constantly, for 2 minutes. Pour in the hot vegetable broth and stir well. Reduce the heat to a simmer and cook, stirring often, for 20–25 minutes, until the broth is reduced and thickened and the rice is al dente.

4 Stir in the zucchini, asparagus, parmesan, lemon juice and remaining butter and season with salt and pepper. Remove from the heat and set aside for 3 minutes. Serve topped with the green onion and mint leaves.

I grew up in the town of Tamworth, NSW, with a father who had a farmer's heart. In the backyard, we always had plenty of chickens for eggs and we grew vegetables and some fruit. My dad always wanted to know what the yearly wheat crop would likely look like out west, so he planted some in the backyard each year. He has kept track of every millimetre of rain that has fallen for decades.

At uni I studied nutrition and dietetics and then did a PhD in biochemistry. I combine my deep appreciation of the land and the food and life it sustains, with the appreciation I have for human health. If farmers stop caring, all health falls apart. **DR LIBBY WEAVER**

brilliant brassica soup

SERVES 4

TIP

Fry some extra broccoli and cauliflower florets in coconut oil to serve on top of the soup.

2 TABLESPOONS COCONUT OIL
   OR GHEE
1 BROWN ONION, FINELY CHOPPED
2 STALKS CELERY, FINELY CHOPPED
2 BROCCOLI HEADS, FLORETS AND
   STALKS ROUGHLY CHOPPED
1 CAULIFLOWER, FLORETS AND STALKS
   ROUGHLY CHOPPED
6 CUPS (1.5 LITRES) HOME-MADE VEGETABLE
   STOCK OR BROTH
400ML COCONUT MILK
⅓ CUP (10G) CHOPPED FRESH FLAT-LEAF
   PARSLEY LEAVES
⅓ CUP (10G) CHOPPED FRESH MINT LEAVES
SEA SALT, TO TASTE

1   Melt the coconut oil or ghee in a large saucepan over medium heat. Add the onion and celery and cook, stirring, for 5 minutes, until soft and translucent.
2   Add the chopped broccoli, cauliflower and stock. Bring to the boil, then reduce the heat and simmer, covered, for 15 minutes, until the vegetables are tender.
3   Stir in the coconut milk and herbs. Season with sea salt and freshly ground black pepper.

3 X 400G CANS WHOLE TOMATOES

1 TABLESPOON OLIVE OIL

1 BROWN ONION, FINELY DICED

SPLASH OF RED WINE

½ TEASPOON GROUND CUMIN

2 LARGE BUNCHES SILVERBEET (ABOUT 700G),
    COARSELY SHREDDED

400G FRESH RICOTTA

100G FETTA

250G INSTANT LASAGNE SHEETS

½ CUP (50G) FINELY GRATED PARMESAN

I'm definitely not a farmer – I grew up in Marrickville, in Sydney's Inner West, where our backyard consisted of a small paved courtyard. After leaving home and spending almost 20 years renting inner-city apartments, I started seeing a man who had grown up on a farm. He had actually killed his own dinner! He took me camping (something I had managed to avoid) and made damper in a billy can. I began to imagine an entirely different life – not on a farm, but maybe somewhere with a garden.

We ended up in Newstead, in regional Victoria. We have a quarter-acre block in a small town of 800 people. Just outside the back door, we've managed to conquer nature and maintain a little vegie patch. I use this term loosely, as the only thing that thrives in this patch is silverbeet. This is one of my many silverbeet recipes. **YASMINE O'SULLIVAN**

silverbeet lasagne

SERVES 6

1   Preheat the oven to 200°C.
2   Purée the canned tomatoes and their juice in a food processor.
3   Heat the olive oil in a large frying pan over medium–high heat. Add the onion and cook for 5–6 minutes, until lightly golden. Stir in the puréed tomatoes, red wine and cumin. Gently simmer for 15 minutes, until the mixture has reduced by about a quarter and thickened slightly.
4   Steam the silverbeet until tender. When cool enough to handle, squeeze the silverbeet with your hands to remove any excess moisture. Combine the silverbeet, ricotta and fetta in a large bowl. Mix until evenly combined.
5   Spread a little of the tomato sauce over the base of a 30cm x 25cm x 5cm ceramic baking dish. Arrange a layer of lasagne sheets over the sauce, breaking to fit, if needed. Cover with a third of the tomato sauce, then a third of the silverbeet mixture. Repeat the layers with the remaining lasagne sheets, sauce and silverbeet mixture. Finish with a layer of tomato sauce. Sprinkle the grated parmesan over the top. Bake for 50–55 minutes, until the lasagne sheets are tender and the top is golden brown.

DAVID & ANDREA MITCHELL

WOOL, SHEEP, CANOLA AND WHEAT FARMERS, MONARO PLAINS, NSW

David Mitchell is driven by a sense of purpose as sharp as the winter winds and snow that whip down the Monaro Plains from the nearby Snowy Mountains. In the shadow of the snowfields, there can be all seasons in one day. It keeps everybody on their toes and reaching for their hat.

Farming, like the weather, waits for no man. It's fulfilling work, but it doesn't come easily. For David and Andrea, the property northwest of Delegate in NSW produces wool, lamb, canola and wheat in some of Australia's toughest conditions. With a long farming history on both sides, David and Andrea knew what they were doing when they bought a soldier settlement block in the early 1990s. With the benefit of David's family owning the adjacent property, there was already 30 years of experience to draw on.

Most of the Mitchells's business has centred around fine-wool growing from merinos. In over 20 years of farming his own place, David has developed a deep connection to the land that he is responsible for and he works hard to ensure it is improved for future generations.

The couple believe that understanding the interaction of soils, pastures, crops, livestock, climate and the interplay of people and finance are extremely complex and essential.

"The skills required to manage these systems and develop world-class products takes knowledge, execution, persistence and integrity," says David. "Persistence and integrity are the key ingredients and the time to make important decisions is early in the drought cycle. The wrong decision can break a family farming business and one of the vital aspects is managing mental health. Living on the Monaro, close to the Snowy Mountains, we are exposed to all elements of the weather – four distinct seasons and sometimes all in one day!" he adds. "I enjoy being confronted by the extremes of the climate. Whether it's an early -6 degree morning bike ride or on a fence line at midday in 40 degrees plus heat, I love it. The most enjoyable part of the job is early morning musters at sunrise. There is nothing like it."

1 CUP (150G) SELF-RAISING FLOUR

½ CUP (75G) PLAIN FLOUR

1 EGG, LIGHTLY WHISKED

1 CUP (250ML) MILK

2 CUPS (400G) DICED LEFT-OVER
    ROAST LAMB

1 SMALL RED ONION, FINELY DICED

¾ CUP (150G) FRESH OR CANNED CORN
    KERNELS

¾ CUP (110G) FROZEN OR CANNED PEAS

3 TEASPOONS BUTTER, MELTED

1 TEASPOON WHITE VINEGAR

VEGETABLE OIL, FOR SHALLOW-FRYING

HOME-MADE TOMATO RELISH OR
    TOMATO SAUCE, TO SERVE

ANDREA MITCHELL'S

lamb fritters

MAKES 6

TIP

You can also use left-over
silverside or roast beef instead
of lamb, and use grated zucchini
or some finely chopped spinach
instead of the peas and corn.

1 Combine the flours and a good pinch of salt in a
large bowl. Pour in the egg and milk. Use a fork
or balloon whisk to mix into a thick batter. Add
the diced lamb, onion, corn, peas and melted
butter and mix until just combined. Stir in the
vinegar. Set aside for 10 minutes before cooking.

2 Preheat the oven to 120°C. Heat the vegetable
oil in a large heavy-based frying over medium–
high heat until hot. Reduce the heat to medium.
Cook the fritters in batches, using ⅓ cup (80ml)
of the batter for each one. Cook for 4–5 minutes,
until bubbles form on the surface. Turn the
fritters over and cook for 4–5 minutes, until
golden and cooked through. Break one fritter
in half to ensure the batter is cooked all the
way through, then adjust the heat and cooking
time accordingly. Keep the fritters warm in
the oven while you cook the remaining batter.

3 Sprinkle the hot fritters with salt and serve
with tomato relish or tomato sauce.

40G BUTTER

500G MIXED MUSHROOMS, THICKLY SLICED

2 SPRIGS THYME

4 CUPS (1 LITRE) BEEF STOCK

½ BROWN ONION, COARSELY CHOPPED

1 STALK CELERY, COARSELY CHOPPED

2 GARLIC CLOVES, COARSELY CHOPPED

2 TABLESPOONS OLIVE OIL

1½ CUPS (330G) ARBORIO RICE

½ CUP (125ML) WHITE WINE (PREFERABLY
  FULL-BODIED CHARDONNAY)

100ML BEEF JUS (OPTIONAL – SEE TIP)

½ CUP (50G) FINELY GRATED
  PARMESAN OR PECORINO

TASMANIA TRUFFLE, FRESHLY SHAVED

My husband Tim and I bought our 15-hectare vineyard, Holm Oak Vineyards, on the banks of the picturesque Tamar River in 2006. Tim is a third-generation viticulturist and we produce a number of varietals, along with the pinot noir that the region is renowned for. We've learned to be flexible in our growing and winemaking approach, because in Tasmania you never know what is going to happen from year to year. Some years will be cooler and drier, some will be hotter, and some will be wetter. You can't make the wine exactly the same way every year. **BEC DUFFY**

mushroom risotto with fresh truffle

SERVES 6

TIP

Beef jus is a reduced beef stock that adds a concentrated flavour. You'll find it at specialty food shops or a good deli. You can leave it out if you can't find it.

1   Melt half the butter in a frying pan over medium–high heat. Cook the mushrooms and thyme, stirring occasionally, for 5 minutes, until the mushrooms are golden and tender. Set aside.

2   Heat the beef stock in a small saucepan and keep hot over low heat.

3   Combine the onion, celery and garlic in a food processor. Process until finely chopped. Heat the olive oil in a large heavy-based saucepan over medium heat. Cook the onion mixture, stirring, for about 3 minutes, until soft.

4   Add the rice and stir for a few minutes until well coated and slightly translucent. Add the wine and cook, stirring, until the wine has evaporated. Add 1 ladle of the hot stock and gently stir until the stock is absorbed. Repeat with the remaining stock, adding 1 ladle at a time and stirring until absorbed after each addition. It will take at least 20 minutes to add all the stock and cook the rice until just tender.

5   Stir in the mushrooms, beef jus, parmesan and remaining butter. Season with pepper, if desired. Divide the risotto among serving plates and top with shaved truffle. Serve with a generous glass of Holm Oak Hotshot Pinot Noir.

ERIKA WATSON & HAYDEN DRUCE

HEIRLOOM PRODUCE, HARTLEY, NSW

P artners in life and work, Erika Watson and Hayden Druce of Epicurean Harvest say they often feel somewhat humbled by the connection they have to the land, managing their property to regenerate soil and plants.

At their farm they grow extraordinary organic heirloom produce, with their business supplying many of the top restaurants in Sydney and the Blue Mountains. But when you get down to it, farming is a hard slog, and when you add the lack of water it's even harder.

With degrees in horticultural science, Erika and Hayden were initially drawn to the land by a shared desire to be a part of a meaningful food system based on an ethic of good agricultural practices. They started by leasing one acre in the Blue Mountains, but since 2016 they've owned 120 acres in Hartley, NSW, where they also manage livestock to regenerate soil, plants and ecology.

Although relative newcomers to the land, their connection to it is deep. "Walking through the paddocks or bush, over creeks or in the rain, listening and feeling the land around you is like going travelling. You learn something new every time, even if they were the same steps you took yesterday," explains Erika.

But no matter how profound their feelings are about it, working their farm is hard graft with a typical day during harvest a race against time.

"We run around picking everything to order, washing and packing to keep it cool for the delivery the next day, as well as managing staff who help us. Delivery is a long day driving into Sydney, visiting restaurant customers, chatting and keeping up to date with what they are doing as well as sharing what's happening on the farm."

Like lots of small businesses they also have to manage their accounts, customers and marketing in their 'downtime'. Plus they're constantly replanting, transplanting, rotating and turning the compost. In between they manage to squeeze in several tea breaks and meals, which are relished, along with lots of patting and playing with the dogs.

Of course, like all farmers they are affected by the drought and also by the disconnection between people and the ecosystems that support the growth of their food. In difficult times they've had to remind themselves to take a breath and ask for help from their community.

When asked what they'd like city folk to understand about what they do, Erika's answer is stark. "[Farming is] in every thought, in every moment. Every step and breath, you live it. It is creative and thoughtful and fun and tiring; we aren't living the dream, we are just living."

Still, they take pleasure in the day-to-day texture of their lives, experiencing small moments with joy and seeing the fruits of their labour on some of the best plates in Australia. And they also get to eat it.

1 TABLESPOON EXTRA VIRGIN OLIVE OIL

2 SMALL SWEET ONIONS (WE GROW

   SHIMONITA AND BARLETTA)

   OR ½ BROWN ONION, CHOPPED

1 GARLIC CLOVE, CHOPPED

½ TEASPOON GRATED LEMON ZEST

½ SMOKED JALEPEÑO CHILLI

   (WE SMOKE THESE AT THE END

   OF SUMMER), FINELY CHOPPED

2CM PIECE GINGER, GRATED

500G PORK MINCE

1 TABLESPOON RICE WINE VINEGAR

1 TABLESPOON TAMARI

1 TABLESPOON HONEY, OR TO TASTE

4 CUPS BRASSICA SHOOTS/LEAVES,

   CHOPPED (SUCH AS CAULIFLOWER,

   BROCCOLI, TURNIP OR KALE)

1 TEASPOON TOASTED SESAME SEEDS

1 TEASPOON SESAME OIL

1 TABLESPOON LEMON JUICE

8 RADICCHIO LEAVES

ERIKA WATSON'S

spring harvest san choy bau

SERVES 4

TIP

This dish is also good served
with black or brown rice.

1 Heat the olive oil in a large frying pan or wok
over high heat. Add the onion and stir-fry for
2–3 minutes, until soft. Add the garlic, lemon
zest, chilli and ginger and stir-fry for 1 minute,
until fragrant. Add the pork mince and stir-fry
for 4–5 minutes, until almost cooked through.

2 Reduce the heat to medium–high and add the
rice wine vinegar, tamari and honey. Stir-fry for
2 minutes, until the pork is cooked through.
Add the brassica shoots and leaves and stir-fry
for 1–2 minutes, until wilted.

3 Transfer the pork mixture to a bowl. Top with
the toasted sesame seeds, sesame oil and lemon
juice. Serve wrapped in radicchio leaves.

RICHARD FAIRLEY

HERB GROWER, BILOELA, QLD

L ife on the land can be a never-ending set of changing challenges – whether it's too little rain, flooding, low prices, oversupply – and a successful modern farmer has to think ahead and plan for the worst, while hoping for the best.

That's been the strategy of growers the Fairley family, who adopted it with great success early in 2000 when they were facing low water levels in the bore water used to irrigate the family lucerne and cotton farm.

Along with five other local farmers, the Fairleys started investigating other crops for the property, specifically more water-efficient options.

"The bores were dropping in yield at the time," explains Richard Fairley. "We heard that herbs were more sustainable, because they are lower in water usage than traditional crops."

Located in Biloela, in Central Queensland, the group of six farmers started growing herbs and selling to various suppliers and retail outlets, until Gourmet Garden, who supply stir-in herb pastes and dried herbs to supermarkets, approached them and an idea was born. Gourmet Garden provided them with a guaranteed supply chain, in return for a commitment to growing herbs – including coriander, basil, continental parsley and oregano.

"Apparently we have the best flavour content they can find," Richard says.

Currently the Fairleys have 140 acres of organically certified land set aside for growing herbs, which is all fully irrigated with bore water. Indeed, the six farmers in the Biloela valley now supply most of the produce for Gourmet Garden, nationally and internationally.

Richard's family was originally from England, with his parents and grandparents migrating to Shepparton in rural Victoria. Richard's parents were keen to establish their own farm, leaving Shepparton and moving to Biloela back in 1986.

"When we went our own way from the grandparents, we moved up here," he says. "We were going to go around Australia, but when we pulled up into little Biloela and looked around, my father fell in love with the place and said it was a good farming area. So we bought a farm, and bought another farm, and just went from there."

Now in partnership with his father ("I'm taking over more and more of the everyday running"), Richard credits his parents, James and Christine, with much of their success and identifying that herbs would be the way to go.

He also feels the same way about the town as his father, he says, and just loves living there.

"For a country town it's got every facility; it's actually brilliant," he adds. "They've got many schools, swimming pools, multiple sporting complexes for kids; the climate's beautiful. It gets a bit hot during summer... but it's still pretty close to the Sunshine Coast and the beach at Yeppoon. It's just a brilliant little country town."

RICHARD FAIRLEY'S

prawn & spring herb spaghetti

SERVES 4

400G DRIED SPAGHETTI

⅓ CUP (80ML) EXTRA VIRGIN OLIVE OIL

2 TABLESPOONS GARLIC PASTE

2 TEASPOONS DRIED CHILLI FLAKES

120G ZUCCHINI FLOWERS OR
    SMALL ZUCCHINI, HALVED

1KG COOKED PRAWNS, PEELED AND
    DEVEINED, TAILS INTACT

4 GREEN ONIONS, THINLY SLICED

1 TABLESPOON LEMON JUICE

½ CUP (10G) SMALL FRESH FLAT-LEAF
    PARSLEY LEAVES, TORN

SEA SALT, TO TASTE

LEMON WEDGES, TO SERVE

1 Cook the spaghetti in a large saucepan of
   boiling salted water until al dente. Drain.

2 Meanwhile, heat 2 tablespoons of the olive
   oil in a small frying pan over medium heat.
   Add the garlic paste and chilli, then remove
   from the heat. Set aside to infuse.

3 Heat the remaining olive oil in a large frying
   pan over medium heat. Add the zucchini and
   cook for 1 minute, until softened. Add the
   prawns, green onion and lemon juice. Cook,
   stirring, for 30 seconds, until the prawns are
   warmed through. Add the garlic and chilli
   mixture and toss until well combined.

4 Divide the pasta among serving bowls or
   plates and top with the zucchini and prawn
   mixture. Scatter the parsley over the top and
   season with sea salt and freshly ground black
   pepper. Serve with lemon wedges.

1 TABLESPOON OLIVE OIL

1 ONION, DICED

700G JAR TOMATO PASSATA

1 TEASPOON DRIED OREGANO

1½ TABLESPOONS CHOPPED FRESH
    FLAT-LEAF PARSLEY

1½ TABLESPOONS SNIPPED FRESH CHIVES

500G FROZEN SPINACH, THAWED

250G RICOTTA

1 EGG, LIGHTLY BEATEN

50G BUTTER

1 GARLIC CLOVE, SLICED

500G BUTTON MUSHROOMS, THINLY SLICED

375G INSTANT LASAGNE SHEETS

1½ CUPS (140G) GRATED PARMESAN

This is a great dish to take to a party. It started life as something different, but my sister and I have changed it so much over the years and we both make it as a weeknight stand-by. It freezes well in large single-serving squares, wrapped in oiled foil packets that are perfect to take out into the paddocks. **BEVERLEY LAING**

ricotta & mushroom lasagne

SERVES 6

TIP

Make sure there's lots of sauce in the dish – it should be quite sloppy. Pour in up to ½ cup (125ml) hot water to prevent the pasta from being claggy.

1 Preheat the oven to 180°C.

2 Heat the olive oil in a saucepan over medium heat. Add the onion and cook, stirring occasionally, until soft. Stir in the passata and herbs. Bring to a simmer, then remove from the heat.

3 Squeeze the spinach to remove most of the liquid, then add to a large bowl. Mix in the ricotta and egg. Season with salt and pepper. Set aside.

4 Melt the butter in a large frying pan over medium–high heat. Cook the garlic for 30 seconds. Add the mushrooms and cook, stirring occasionally, for 5 minutes, until just tender. Season with salt and pepper. Set aside.

5 Grease a 25cm x 20cm x 5cm ovenproof dish. Spread a little of the tomato sauce over the base. Arrange a layer of lasagne sheets over the sauce, breaking to fit, if needed. Cover with a third of the tomato sauce. Spread a third of the ricotta mixture over the top, then another layer of lasagne sheets, followed by half the mushrooms.

6 Continue layering, finishing with the ricotta mixture. Sprinkle the grated parmesan over the top. Place the dish on a baking tray and bake for 45 minutes, until the pasta is tender and the top is golden brown.

DAVID CHUNG

MARKET GARDENER, AUSTRAL, NSW

Expectations were different for teenagers back in 1961 when David Chung migrated to Australia from Hong Kong. At just 13 years of age and with only a couple of years of English, he travelled alone and left his family behind, staying with friends who were operating a small farm in Chipping Norton, in Sydney's western suburbs.

After finishing his schooling, he spent time learning about farming before deciding to buy his own patch of land in Austral, NSW, to grow Asian greens – bok choy, choi sum, baby bok choy, green onions and coriander – firstly for the local Chinese market, then for the rest of the country as people started cooking stir-fries as an everyday meal.

"I didn't really want to go into farming," David, now 70, explains, "but my father said to stay on the farm. He could see that while farming is hard work, you got a lot of free time. He told me that when you get married and you have children, it helps to have free time."

Like many Chinese-born Australians, David also tried his hand at the restaurant business, but decided that his father was right and that farming was the way to go when you have a growing family. "If the kids are sick you can't close the restaurant," he says. "My wife depended on me. So I stayed with the farming."

And, while farming can be hard work, David says he wouldn't have it any other way.

"The weather can be hot, windy or wet," he says, "but I always tell people that if you do farming you will be satisfied. I get up at 7am; I finish at 8pm. It is hard work, but I stay where I am."

It is a business that sustains the whole Chung family. David's 98-year-old father still lives on the property, although he no longer works in the business. David and his two sons now employ labourers in the fields, while working mostly in the Sydney Produce Markets selling their vegetables to providores and restaurants.

"I can retire now, but why stop work unless you have to?" he asks. "I do a couple of days to help the boys. I go overseas three or four times a year. It's a good life, I can't ask for any more."

The drought has affected the Chung family farm greatly. Because Asian greens require a lot of water, David needs to use the mains water to top up his dam – in recent months he's faced bills of $8000 a quarter for water. While the fields of vegetables look green because of all the irrigation, the vegetable beds are surrounded by brown fields and dry dams.

As a small-scale farmer, David feels that his type of agriculture often gets overlooked when it comes to drought relief – images of large outback cattle or sheep stations tend to be the dominant vernacular of Australian rural life, not small market gardens on the outskirts of the city.

"Everybody in the city basin is five or 10 acres," he says. "We are a bit different."

Not that he would change a thing. "I like Australia," he says. "It's a good country. I have travelled around and I can't see anywhere I would rather be. It's changed, but it's still better than any other country."

DAVID CHUNG'S

beef & asian greens stir-fry

SERVES 4

2 TABLESPOONS PEANUT OIL

500G RUMP STEAK, CUT INTO THIN STRIPS

1 BROWN ONION, THINLY SLICED

1 TABLESPOON GRATED FRESH GINGER

1 BUNCH BOK CHOY, ROUGHLY CHOPPED

200G SNOW PEAS

1 BUNCH BROCCOLINI, ROUGHLY CHOPPED

2 TABLESPOONS OYSTER SAUCE

1 TEASPOON SESAME OIL

STEAMED RICE, TO SERVE

1   Heat half the peanut oil in a wok over high heat. Stir-fry the beef until browned. Remove from the wok. Wipe the wok clean.

2   Heat the remaining peanut oil in the wok over high heat. Stir-fry the sliced onion for 5 minutes, until soft. Add the ginger and stir-fry for 2 minutes, until fragrant.

3   Add the bok choy, snow peas, broccolini, oyster sauce and sesame oil. Stir-fry for 3 minutes, until the vegetables are bright green and just tender. Return the beef to the wok and stir-fry for 3 minutes.

4   Serve immediately, with steamed rice.

2KG BONED PORK LOIN WITH RIND

3 TEASPOONS FENNEL SEEDS

1 TEASPOON DRIED CHILLI FLAKES

1 TEASPOON SEA SALT FLAKES

1 TABLESPOON EXTRA VIRGIN OLIVE OIL

4 FRESH BAY LEAVES

6 LARGE FRESH SAGE LEAVES

JUICE OF 1 LEMON

SALT, FOR RUBBING

During the late 1980s, I worked as the food consultant and stylist for the Australian Pork Corporation. We promoted Australian pork on television food shows, in recipe leaflets, on radio and in magazine campaigns. I had the opportunity to work closely with butchers who were very passionate about Australian farmers and pig producers. It was very important to me to educate people through my recipes that pork didn't require the long cooking times that came from the kitchens of England. It wasn't an easy message, but we persisted in saying that pork is much more delicious when just cooked through and is perfectly 'food safe to eat slightly pink'. **ANNA PHILLIPS**

porchetta

SERVES 6–8

TIPS

For the best crackling, allow the uncovered pork to stand in the fridge overnight to dry out the rind.
The pan juices can be used to make a delicious gravy.

1   Preheat the oven to 240°C.
2   Score the pork rind with a sharp knife (or ask your butcher to do it for you). Lay the pork on a board, rind-side down, and open it out flat.
3   Use a mortar and pestle to grind the fennel seeds, chilli flakes and sea salt flakes. Drizzle the pork flesh with the olive oil and scatter the fennel mixture over the top. Lay the bay leaves and sage leaves along the centre of the pork. Firmly roll up the pork and secure it with kitchen string.
4   Place the pork on a wire rack in a roasting tin. Pour the lemon juice over the scored rind and rub in well. Sprinkle liberally with salt, rubbing it into the rind. Roast the pork for 20 minutes, until the rind begins to crackle. Reduce the oven to 180°C. Cook for a further 1½–2 hours, until cooked to your liking. Serve the pork with roast potato, pumpkin and zucchini, and gravy (see Tips).

2 TABLESPOONS OLIVE OIL

2 TABLESPOONS FRESH THYME LEAVES

2 GARLIC CLOVES, CRUSHED

1.4KG LAMB LEG, BONE IN

¾ CUP (185ML) LAMB OR BEEF STOCK

700G KIPFLER POTATOES, SCRUBBED, HALVED

GRATED ZEST OF 1 LEMON

3 CUPS (450G) FROZEN PEAS

20G BUTTER, CHOPPED

1 BUNCH MINT, LEAVES STRIPPED,
FINELY CHOPPED, PLUS EXTRA
MINT SPRIGS TO SERVE

1 TABLESPOON CASTER SUGAR

⅓ CUP (80ML) BOILING WATER

⅓ CUP (80ML) WHITE VINEGAR

Coming from a long line of graziers, my nan, Leila Mayoh, was a true woman of the land. She single-handedly kept our farm, Karoola Estate, at Roslyn, in the Southern Highlands of NSW, running during World War II while Pa was off fighting.

To this day, the smell of mint immediately transports me to Nan's garden near the outdoor laundry, where the brown snakes lived. She would have used lard saved from roasts gone by, instead of olive oil, and everyday spuds in her roast. She lives on in my heart and my cooking forever. **SARAH MAYOH**

nan's roast lamb with fresh mint sauce

SERVES 6

1 Combine 1 tablespoon of the olive oil with the thyme and garlic in a small bowl. Season with salt and pepper.

2 Preheat the oven to 180°C. Place the lamb in a large roasting tin and brush with the thyme mixture. Pour the stock around the base of the lamb. Cover with foil and roast for 1 hour, then remove the foil and roast the lamb for a further 20–30 minutes, until cooked to your liking.

3 Meanwhile, put the potatoes on a large baking tray lined with baking paper. Drizzle with the remaining olive oil and sprinkle with the lemon zest. Season and toss to coat. Add to the oven with the lamb and roast for 35–40 minutes, until golden and tender.

4 Set the lamb aside, covered with foil, for 15 minutes to rest. Reserve any pan juices.

5 Cook the peas in a saucepan of boiling water for 5 minutes, until tender. Drain and return to the pan. Add the butter, season and toss to coat. Keep warm.

6 Place the chopped mint, sugar and a good pinch of salt in a jug. Stir in the boiling water, then set aside to cool. Once cooled, stir in the vinegar. Taste and adjust the seasoning.

7 Slice the lamb and drizzle with any pan juices. Serve with the potatoes, peas, mint sauce and extra mint sprigs.

3KG BONED PORK SHOULDER

1 TABLESPOON OLIVE OIL

2 TABLESPOONS SMOKED PAPRIKA

2 TABLESPOONS GROUND CUMIN

2 TABLESPOONS BROWN SUGAR

800ML CIDER OR APPLE JUICE

SMOKY BARBECUE SAUCE

2 ORANGES

1 LARGE ONION, PEELED

5 GARLIC CLOVES

2 RED CHILLIES

¼ CUP (7G) FRESH THYME

2 TABLESPOONS FRESH ROSEMARY LEAVES

2 BAY LEAVES

⅓ CUP (35G) SMOKED PAPRIKA

1 TABLESPOON GROUND CUMIN

1 TABLESPOON OLIVE OIL

1 CUP (185G) BROWN SUGAR

100ML APPLE JUICE

200ML TOMATO SAUCE

100ML WORCESTERSHIRE SAUCE

¼ CUP (60ML) BALSAMIC VINEGAR

2 TEASPOONS DIJON MUSTARD

My wife and I live on a small farm overlooking the Bega Valley. It's very hard work and at times it's a heartbreaking struggle. The reward is food on a table that gives life, not just nourishment; it fosters togetherness and gratitude, and brings love to the fore even in the toughest of times.

STEVE JACKSON

pulled pork with smoky barbecue sauce

SERVES 6-8

TIP

Any remaining barbecue sauce can be refrigerated for up to 2 weeks.

1 Preheat the oven to 150°C. Rub the pork all over with the olive oil. Combine the paprika, cumin and brown sugar and season generously with salt and cracked black pepper. Place the pork in a baking dish, skin-side up. Rub all over with the spice mixture. Pour the cider or apple juice into the dish. Cover with foil and bake for 4–8 hours, until falling apart.

2 Meanwhile, to make the barbecue sauce, put the oranges in a saucepan of water. Simmer for 1 hour, until soft. Transfer the oranges to a food processor and blitz to a pulp. Remove and set aside.

3 Blitz the onion, garlic, red chillies, thyme, rosemary, bay leaves, paprika and cumin in a food processor.

4 Heat the oil in a large saucepan over medium heat. Sauté the herb and spice mixture for 2 minutes. Add the brown sugar and stir until dissolved. Add the orange pulp, apple juice, tomato sauce, Worcestershire sauce, balsamic vinegar and mustard. Bring to the boil, then reduce the heat and simmer for 10 minutes. Remove from the heat and set aside to cool.

5 Remove the skin from the pork and shred the meat with two forks, incorporating the pan juices. Stir in 1–2 cups (250–500ml) of the barbecue sauce. Serve the pork on crusty white rolls with aioli-dressed coleslaw.

4–5 LARGE CARROTS, PEELED,
    COARSELY GRATED
1 LARGE HANDFUL OF FRESH MINT LEAVES
1 SMALL HANDFUL OF FRESH CORIANDER
    LEAVES
1 BEETROOT, PEELED INTO RIBBONS
1 CUP (160G) TAMARI ALMONDS,
    COARSELY CHOPPED

DRESSING
1 LONG RED CHILLI, DESEEDED,
    FINELY CHOPPED
1 TEASPOON FINELY GRATED FRESH GINGER
1 TEASPOON SUMAC
⅓ CUP (80ML) GOOD-QUALITY
    EXTRA VIRGIN OLIVE OIL
1–2 TABLESPOONS LEMON JUICE
1 TABLESPOON APPLE CIDER VINEGAR
½ CUP (75G) CURRANTS

My first connection with the land is a memory from my childhood: not a farm in the country, but a vegie garden in the suburbs. I've always had our family food garden as a clear, fond memory, and that's exactly what I want for my kids. When I see my kids eating cherry tomatoes from the plant or snapping off a snow pea, it makes me smile. I'm all about buying local, supporting farmers' markets and organic food choices. My kids meet the farmers. It helps them conceptualise our family footprint on this earth and how we can reduce it simply by choosing local Australian produce. **BECKY SEARLES**

rainbow salad

SERVES 4 AS A SIDE

1 To make the dressing, combine the ingredients in a bowl. Set aside for 30 minutes to allow the currants to soften slightly. Season with salt and freshly ground black pepper.
2 Toss the carrot, mint and coriander in a bowl. Transfer to a serving platter alongside the beetroot and top with the chopped almonds.
3 Gently toss the salad with the dressing just before serving.

ANNA JEWELL

RICE GROWER, FIELD OFFICER, FINLEY, NSW

Anna Jewell was always her dad's right-hand girl. Fourth-generation farmer Anna would sometimes wave to the school bus from the stockyards instead of boarding it, so an agricultural science degree was a natural progression.

Based in Finley in NSW's southern Riverina, Anna is an agronomic field officer with Sunrice; a rice growers' co-op with 2200 employees, 30 brands and a broad international reach. When she's not out in the field with the growers, she relaxes at home with her husband and business partner (and fellow fourth-generation farmer), Scott. She says her off-farm work of supporting growers to achieve productive results helps inform her own farming decisions.

Anna's favourite part of rice farming is being out there checking the crops, seeing how they're growing, watching them change and checking the water levels during the summer growing months. She says the water trickling over the stops into the next bay is as calming as the sound of it gushing when they are reopened. "Rice creates a nice ecosystem that cools the dry Riverina plains," she explains.

With a dry summer forecast, the Mallee topsoil will be dragged away on hot westerly winds, so keeping the yard at home green is important to Anna and Scott. They believe the garden must be a refuge and there should be no drought inside the garden fence.

"Lack of rain and irrigation water availability is definitely the biggest threat to our income," says Anna. "Rice is our most profitable crop when we are able to grow it. We have had to get smarter and more efficient in our growing methods. We now flush our paddocks by turning the water on and off between the October planting window and Christmas. After that we flood permanently until harvest in early autumn. Australians are the most efficient rice growers in the world, using the least water and other crop inputs compared to our global colleagues. Our water usage can be regulated to 0.1 of a megalitre at the touch of our smart phones."

Around 30 per cent of Australian rice is consumed domestically and the rest is exported. A premium product marketed to a discerning global customer base, Australian rice also guarantees that what is on the label is in the packet.

Clearly, 2018 outstrips the driest years of the last decade. Only 10 kilometres north, the crops have already died.

"We have each other and the extended family," says Anna. "It's really important to stay optimistic, be proactive in our decision-making, make joint decisions and to support each other so neither one feels like they're shouldering the full burden of those decisions. The decisions that we make daily can have a significant effect on our livelihoods. It can make or break us at the drop of a hat. That's why it's so important to share the burden and stay focused."

For Anna, the small farming community brings a communal acceptance of the challenges that farmers face. Knowing they are providing a vital service putting meals on the table makes it all worthwhile, she says. As long as there is water.

ANNA JEWELL'S

vegetable curry

SERVES 6
——————

2 TEASPOONS VEGETABLE OIL

2 TABLESPOONS MADRAS CURRY PASTE

1 CUP (250ML) VEGETABLE STOCK

400ML LIGHT COCONUT CREAM

1 RED CAPSICUM, CHOPPED

1KG PUMPKIN, PEELED, CUT INTO 2CM PIECES

1 SMALL CAULIFLOWER (750G), TRIMMED,
    CUT INTO FLORETS

3 TOMATOES, ROUGHLY CHOPPED

300G GREEN BEANS, TRIMMED, HALVED

400G CAN CHICKPEAS, RINSED, DRAINED

1 CUP (260G) GREEK-STYLE PLAIN YOGHURT

1 LEBANESE CUCUMBER, FINELY CHOPPED

2 TABLESPOONS CHOPPED FRESH CORIANDER
    LEAVES, PLUS EXTRA CORIANDER LEAVES
    TO SERVE

1 CUP (220G) SUNRICE MEDIUM GRAIN
    RICE, COOKED ACCORDING TO PACKET
    DIRECTIONS

1   Heat the oil in a large saucepan over medium heat. Add the curry paste and cook, stirring, for 30 seconds, until fragrant. Pour in the vegetable stock and bring to a simmer.

2   Stir in the coconut cream, capsicum and pumpkin. Cover and cook for 10 minutes, until the pumpkin is just tender. Add the cauliflower and tomato. Cook for 10 minutes, then add the beans and chickpeas and cook for a further 5 minutes, until the beans are just tender.

3   Combine the yoghurt and cucumber with the chopped coriander in a small bowl.

4   Garnish the curry with the extra coriander and serve with the rice and yoghurt mixture.

Growing food and connecting with the soil and seasons is a most magical and meaningful thing to do, and I encourage everyone to grow as much as they can in their own spaces.

MORAG GAMBLE

eggy bakes

SERVES 4

TIP

Try adding some chopped steamed vegetables or grated tasty cheese or ricotta to the egg mixture.

6 EGGS

¼ CUP (60ML) MILK

½ CUP (15G) MIXED FRESH HERBS, SUCH AS
    OREGANO, THYME, ROSEMARY, BASIL,
    VIETNAMESE MINT, CORIANDER OR
    GARLIC CHIVES

¼ CUP (50G) CORN KERNELS

¼ CUP (40G) FROZEN PEAS

1 BUNCH SEASONAL GARDEN GREENS,
    SUCH AS BROCCOLINI, PUMPKIN LEAVES,
    SWEET POTATO LEAVES, SPINACH, SORREL,
    PURSLANE, KALE, MUSTARD GREENS,
    CHINESE GREENS OR BEETROOT LEAVES

1 Preheat the oven to 180°C. Grease six 1 cup (250ml) pie tins or ramekins and place on a baking tray.
2 Place the eggs, milk and herbs into a bowl and whisk to combine. Season with salt and pepper. Pour into the prepared dishes. Top with the corn, peas and seasonal greens.
3 Bake for 15–20 minutes, until set.

350G ZUCCHINI

PINCH OF SEA SALT FLAKES

100ML EXTRA VIRGIN OLIVE OIL

3 FREE-RANGE EGGS

GRATED ZEST OF 1 LEMON

2 CUPS (300G) SELF-RAISING FLOUR

½ TEASPOON BICARBONATE
  OF SODA

2 TABLESPOONS RAW SUGAR

PINCH OF GROUND CINNAMON

PINCH OF FRESHLY GRATED NUTMEG

200G SOFT MARINATED FETTA

100G SLICED SALAMI

PICKLES

1¼ CUPS (310ML) WHITE WINE VINEGAR

1½ CUPS (300G) CASTER SUGAR

PINCH OF SAFFRON THREADS

PINCH OF DRIED CHILLI FLAKES

1 FENNEL BULB, TRIMMED, HALVED, THINLY
  SLICED

1 SALAD ONION OR WHITE ONION, HALVED,
  THINLY SLICED

1 CARROT, THINLY SLICED

I was head chef at Circa in St Kilda, but I felt disconnected from the food I was cooking: lots of middle men, meats coming on a truck from Sydney, cheeses from around the world, fruit and vegetables eaten out of season. A visit to farmers Brendan and Kate Eisner at Daylesford Organics set me on course to buying local, direct from farmers. **MATT WILKINSON**

zucchini bread

SERVES 6–8

This is an edited extract from *Mr & Mrs Wilkinson's How It Is At Home* by Matt Wilkinson and Sharlee Gibb, published by Hardie Grant Books.

1 Preheat the oven to 180°C. Lightly grease and flour a 6cm-deep, 24cm x 12cm loaf tin.

2 Coarsely grate the zucchini. Combine with the salt in a bowl and set aside for 10 minutes. Rinse and drain the zucchini, then squeeze out the excess moisture. Transfer to a bowl.

3 Stir the olive oil, eggs and lemon zest into the zucchini. Combine the flour, bicarbonate of soda, sugar and spices in a separate bowl. Fold into the zucchini mixture until combined.

4 Pour the batter into the tin and bake for 50–70 minutes, until a skewer inserted into the centre comes out clean. Cool in the tin for 10 minutes. Turn out onto a wire rack to cool.

5 To make the pickles, put the vinegar, sugar, saffron, chilli and 300ml water in a saucepan over medium heat. Bring to the boil. Put the fennel, onion and carrot in a large sterilised jar. Pour the hot vinegar mixture over the vegetables. Leave to cool.

6 To serve, slice the zucchini bread and smear it with fetta. Top with the salami and pickles.

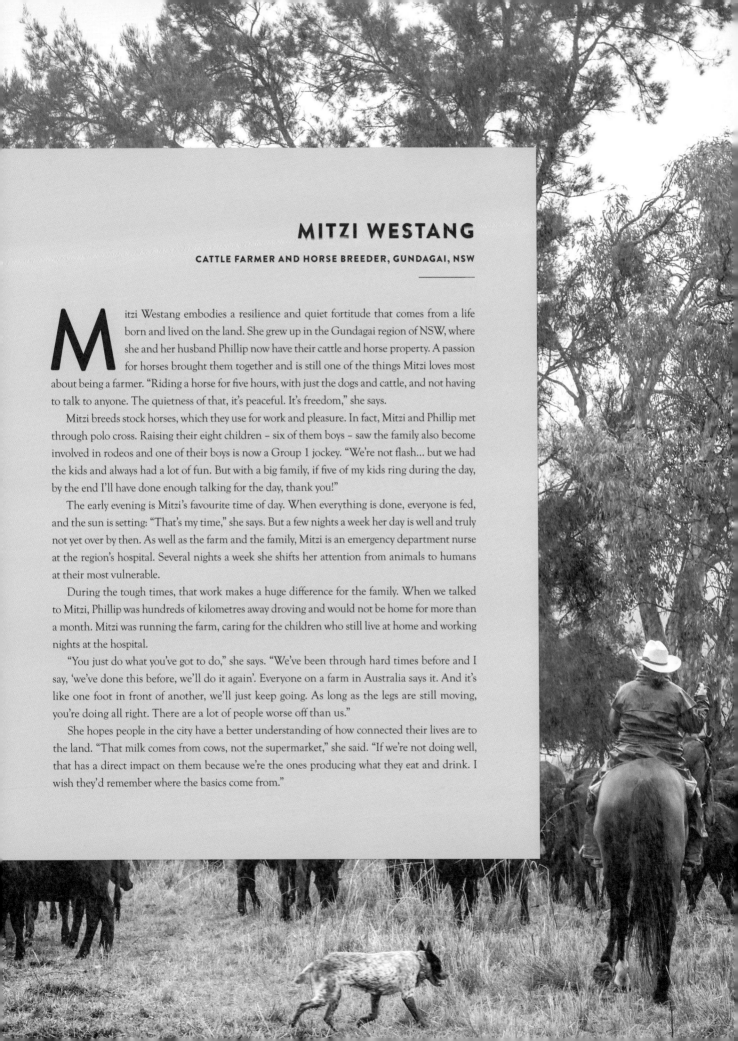

MITZI WESTANG

CATTLE FARMER AND HORSE BREEDER, GUNDAGAI, NSW

———

Mitzi Westang embodies a resilience and quiet fortitude that comes from a life born and lived on the land. She grew up in the Gundagai region of NSW, where she and her husband Phillip now have their cattle and horse property. A passion for horses brought them together and is still one of the things Mitzi loves most about being a farmer. "Riding a horse for five hours, with just the dogs and cattle, and not having to talk to anyone. The quietness of that, it's peaceful. It's freedom," she says.

Mitzi breeds stock horses, which they use for work and pleasure. In fact, Mitzi and Phillip met through polo cross. Raising their eight children – six of them boys – saw the family also become involved in rodeos and one of their boys is now a Group 1 jockey. "We're not flash... but we had the kids and always had a lot of fun. But with a big family, if five of my kids ring during the day, by the end I'll have done enough talking for the day, thank you!"

The early evening is Mitzi's favourite time of day. When everything is done, everyone is fed, and the sun is setting: "That's my time," she says. But a few nights a week her day is well and truly not yet over by then. As well as the farm and the family, Mitzi is an emergency department nurse at the region's hospital. Several nights a week she shifts her attention from animals to humans at their most vulnerable.

During the tough times, that work makes a huge difference for the family. When we talked to Mitzi, Phillip was hundreds of kilometres away droving and would not be home for more than a month. Mitzi was running the farm, caring for the children who still live at home and working nights at the hospital.

"You just do what you've got to do," she says. "We've been through hard times before and I say, 'we've done this before, we'll do it again'. Everyone on a farm in Australia says it. And it's like one foot in front of another, we'll just keep going. As long as the legs are still moving, you're doing all right. There are a lot of people worse off than us."

She hopes people in the city have a better understanding of how connected their lives are to the land. "That milk comes from cows, not the supermarket," she said. "If we're not doing well, that has a direct impact on them because we're the ones producing what they eat and drink. I wish they'd remember where the basics come from."

MITZI WESTANG'S

meatloaf

SERVES 6–8

1KG LEAN BEEF MINCE

1½ CUPS (90G) FRESH BREADCRUMBS
    OR TORN STALE BREAD

1 ONION, FINELY GRATED

1 CARROT, FINELY GRATED

2 TABLESPOONS CHOPPED FRESH
    FLAT-LEAF PARSLEY LEAVES

1 TABLESPOON CHOPPED FRESH
    ROSEMARY LEAVES, PLUS EXTRA
    SPRIGS TO GARNISH

1 EGG, LIGHTLY BEATEN

2 TEASPOONS WORCESTERSHIRE SAUCE

1 TABLESPOON DIJON MUSTARD

¾ CUP (185ML) TOMATO SAUCE

¼ CUP (90G) HONEY

1 Preheat the oven to 180°C. Grease a 20cm x 10cm loaf tin and line the base.

2 Put the mince, breadcrumbs, onion, carrot, herbs, egg, Worcestershire sauce and mustard into a bowl and mix to combine. Press the mixture into the loaf tin.

3 Combine the tomato sauce and honey in a bowl. Brush half the mixture over the top of the meatloaf. Bake for 20 minutes. Remove from the oven and brush with the remaining tomato and honey mixture. Top with the rosemary sprigs and return to the oven for 25 minutes, until cooked through.

4 Serve the meatloaf in slices with a leafy green salad. Meatloaf is fantastic on sandwiches – meatloaf and tomato sauce sandwiches are the perfect road trip lunch!

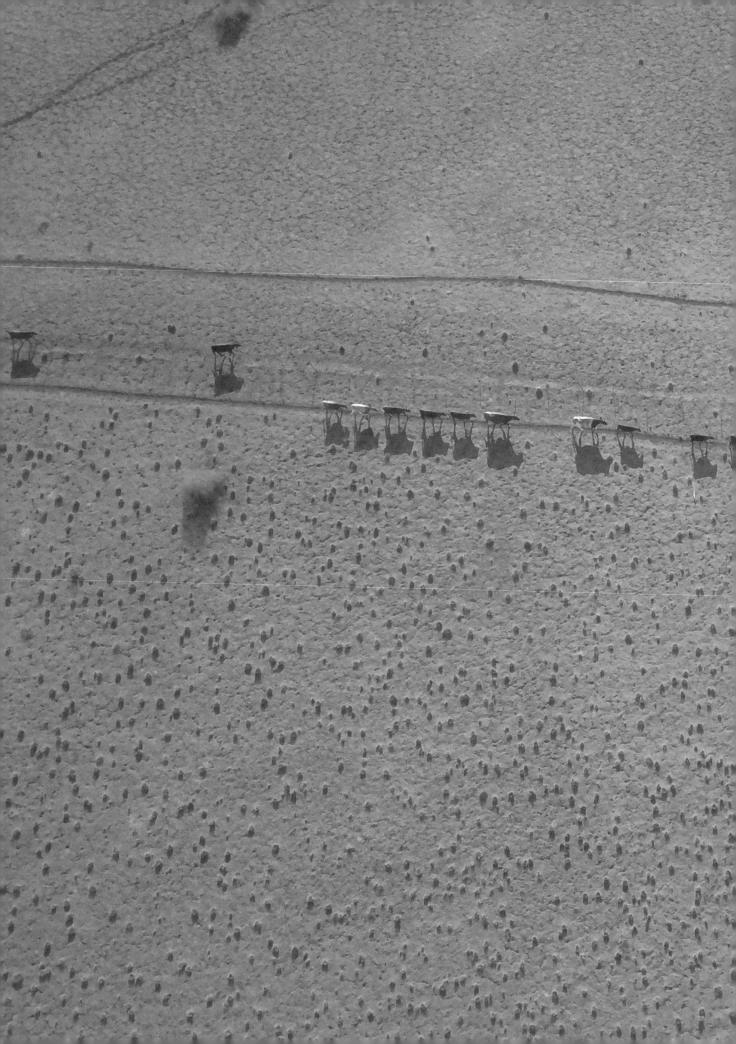

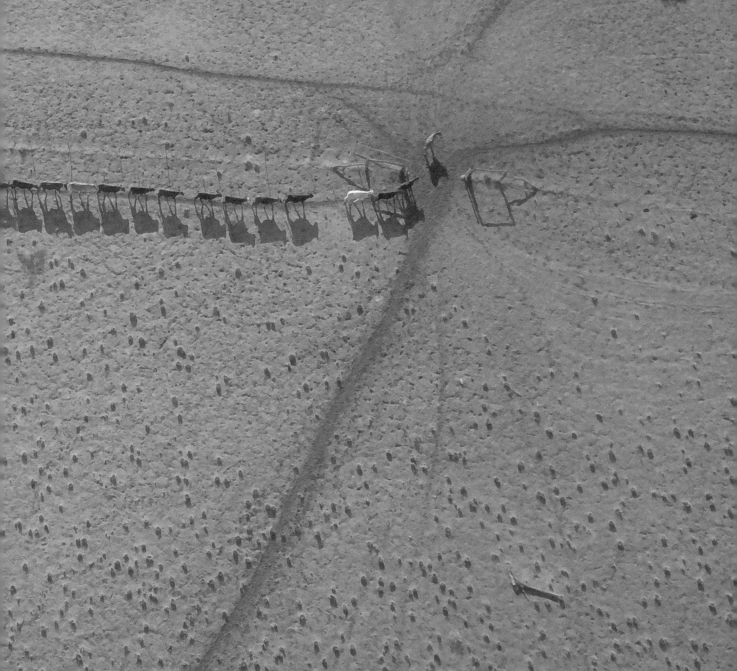

SWEET STUFF

JANE SMITH

FARMER, BAKER, VEGETABLE GROWER AND BLOGGER

A love of food and an interest in photography grew into a popular blog about wholesome country pleasures for Jane Smith, who lives on a station east of Broken Hill with her husband Terry and two children. As the caretaker of the property's extensive vegetable garden, she believes in eating with the seasons, cooking from scratch and minimising waste.

Jane's family's farming history goes back several generations and she and Terry have lived on their current property for almost 19 years.

"I love that I'm constantly surrounded by natural beauty," says Jane. "We have endless horizons, red dirt, blue skies and freedom that many people can only dream of. Even during the driest, hottest times when the landscape is harsh and unforgiving, I can still see the beauty in the light and in the hardy plants and animals."

A typical day in the Smith household starts at 6am, with ABC radio and breakfast before the children get up. Jane often prepares food for employees, checks the vegetable garden or feeds the pets, "always with the reassuring sound of my coffee machine warming up".

"On a typical day, in between taking care of our children, I might deliver food to the paddock for my husband and his work crew, or I might drive around our network of water tanks and troughs, checking for any problems," she adds. "My tasks depend on the season and what part of the farming cycle we happen to be in."

While life out west can be tough, Jane says she believes in resilience.

"I gain strength from my supportive husband, family and friends," she says. "I also have some side projects away from farming, such as my blog, The Shady Baker, food writing and bread baking. These ventures keep me connected with a different community, provide me with a creative outlet and add another positive dimension to my overall wellbeing."

Jane says she relishes the independence of life on the land and the ability to raise her children in wide, open spaces. "Our children have a solid understanding of where their food comes from, a strong work ethic and a sense of responsibility for the land and our animals," she says. "Living off the land keeps us closely connected to the cycle of life, both the triumphant times and the heartbreaking times."

1 CUP (250ML) MILK, WARMED TO AROUND 30°C

150G BUTTER, MELTED

⅓ CUP (75G) CASTER SUGAR

7G SACHET DRIED YEAST

1 EGG

1 TEASPOON SALT

4 CUPS (600 G) PLAIN FLOUR

100G DARK CHOCOLATE,
    FINELY CHOPPED

½ CUP (160G) ORANGE MARMALADE

JANE SMITH'S

dark chocolate scrolls

MAKES 8

1 Combine the warm milk, melted butter and caster sugar in the bowl of a stand mixer or a large bowl. Add the yeast and stand for 5 minutes without mixing.

2 Add the egg, salt and half of the flour and mix in using a dough hook attachment or by hand. Add the remaining flour and mix until the dough forms a smooth ball, about 6–7 minutes.

3 Transfer the dough to a lightly greased bowl, cover and leave in a warm place for 3 hours, until doubled in size.

4 Line a 24cm round cake tin with baking paper.

5 Roll out the dough to a rectangle approximately 30cm x 17cm and 2cm thick. Cut it lengthways into eight strips, about 3cm wide and sprinkle a thin layer of chocolate over each strip. Carefully roll up each strip to form a spiral and neatly pack into the cake tin, leaving 3–4cm between each. Sprinkle any extra chocolate over the top. Cover with plastic wrap and refrigerate overnight.

6 Remove the buns from the refrigerator and set aside in a warm place for 2 hours.

7 Preheat the oven to 200°C. Bake the scrolls for 20–25 minutes, until dark golden in colour.

8 Heat the marmalade in a small saucepan over medium–high heat. Strain through a fine sieve, then brush over the warm scrolls. Serve warm.

BLACK AND GOLD KELPIE

WORKING DOGS

My name is Frank but they call me the car dog. If someone's going somewhere – anywhere – I want to be included and jump in for the ride. There's always at least one dog with our owner, Terry. Growing up, my first memories were of waking up at the crack of dawn and jumping on the back of a motorbike or riding in the ute with Terry or one of the other boys. Our training takes a good two years of going out every single day with the crew. Watching, learning, letting our instincts take over.

During the first couple of years of a pup's life, a special bond is formed with their owner, like a lifelong partnership between mates or family. And when we're out on the land, we need that unbreakable bond in order to work together and get the job done.

I've been herding merino sheep and Hereford cattle for as long as I can remember. Between you and me, I'm actually a bit scared of the old things. Well, more specifically the rams – I had a bad experience once, got trapped up against the gate with an angry ram. Not a good spot to get stuck, what with their horns coming at you and your back up against the wall. These days I know how to communicate with them a bit better and I know which ones to leave alone.

I came to Terry and Jane about nine years ago. I was just a pup and they also had my brother. But now I'm the oldest in the pack and I'm the leader. The younger dogs look up to me and everything they know about mustering and working the land is because of me and Terry. When we're out working, they'll watch what I do and follow my lead.

It has always been me and Terry. We've shared a lot of good moments and I try to make him laugh as much as I can. People think we're just working dogs but we actually have a lot of character. When us kelpies form that loyal bond with an owner, nothing can break it and I'd never work for anyone else except in rare cases. I have one rare case – Terry's 12-year-old daughter, Annabelle. Sometimes she'll come out and work with us. The girl sure knows how to ride a bike and muster. When she's not rounding up and moving livestock with us, she's putting us farm dogs through an obstacle course that she set up herself. I don't love doing it, especially after a 10-hour day out in the full sun, but I have a soft spot for Annabelle so I play along. I prefer it when my mate Digger is about because he loves jumping through her hoops and I'm happy for him to be the show pony.

Nowadays, after earning my stripes with Terry, I work the shed and the yard and the other dogs get the big mustering jobs. I get special treatment because I'm Terry's favourite. I don't have to sleep out like the other dogs anymore. It's a nice privilege to have in my older years and I usually give the other dogs a cheeky grin as I pass them on my way in.

My parents had an organic orchard in central west NSW. They raised my sisters and me to have a deep respect for the Australian landscape, to be very conscious of food waste and to only take from the land what we need. Mum was always preserving, pickling and dehydrating anything that might go to waste. I understand now that this was not just about food waste, it was also about how hard Mum and Dad had worked to grow every apple, every pear, every peach. They thought about how much water they used, how to keep the soil sustainable, and how much they should pick every week to sell. Now is the time for us to take care of our farmers, and show our support by knowing our producers and their stories. **PHOEBE WOOD**

apple & rosemary tart

SERVES 6

———————

375G ALL-BUTTER PUFF PASTRY, THAWED

50G UNSALTED BUTTER, SOFTENED

⅔ CUP (70G) ALMOND MEAL

1 EGG YOLK

1 TEASPOON VANILLA BEAN PASTE

200ML HONEY, WARMED

2 PINK LADY APPLES, THINLY SLICED

1 SPRIG ROSEMARY

DOUBLE CREAM, TO SERVE

1 Preheat the oven to 200°C.

2 Roll out the pastry between two sheets of baking paper to a 30cm round with a thickness of 3mm. Remove the top sheet of paper and lift the pastry onto a baking tray.

3 Combine the butter, almond meal, egg yolk, vanilla and ¼ cup (60ml) of the honey in a small bowl. Beat with a wooden spoon until smooth. Spread the mixture over the pastry circle. Arrange the apple slices on top and drizzle with another ¼ cup (60ml) of honey. Bake the tart for 20 minutes, until golden and crisp.

4 Combine the remaining honey and the rosemary leaves in a small saucepan over low heat. Swirl to melt the honey. Drizzle over the tart. Serve the tart with cream.

500G MILK ARROWROOT BISCUITS

500G UNSALTED BUTTER, CHOPPED

⅔ CUP (160ML) MILK

¼ CUP (30G) COCOA POWDER

500G CASTER SUGAR

ICING

300G MILK CHOCOLATE, CHOPPED

¾ CUP (180ML) THICKENED CREAM

40G UNSALTED BUTTER

When I moved to the far north coast of NSW in 2011, the sense of community in a smaller town and more rural environment had a fast and ultimately everlasting effect on me. Byron Bay is lucky to share the beauty of both ocean and country. People here know each other, look out for each other and make an effort to support each other. I quickly found the local farmers' markets and by the time Jeremy and I opened 100 Mile Table cafe, chatting with local farmers, growers and suppliers was our default. It is a privilege to now call so many local farmers and producers friends. It's so important for us as consumers to understand the good times and bad times, the highs and lows that people on the land face. Thank you to the farmers. We'd be nowhere without you. **SARAH SWAN**

nana's bakeless cake

MAKES 24 PIECES

1   Grease a deep 30cm x 20cm cake tin. Line the base and sides, with the paper extending 5cm above the edge.

2   Process the biscuits in a food processor to the texture of very coarse crumbs. Transfer to a large bowl.

3   Place the butter, milk, cocoa and sugar in a small saucepan over medium heat. Bring to the boil, then reduce to a very gentle simmer and cook for 30 seconds, until the sugar has dissolved. Pour the mixture over the biscuit crumbs. Mix well.

4   Pour the mixture into the prepared tin and press firmly until it is evenly spread. Leave to cool for 15 minutes, then cover and refrigerate for 4 hours, until firm.

5   To make the icing, combine the chocolate, cream and butter in a heatproof bowl over a saucepan of simmering water. Stir constantly until the mixture has melted and is smooth. Set aside to cool slightly, then pour over the cake and smooth the surface. Refrigerate overnight or until set.

6   Remove the cake from the tin and cut into squares to serve.

3 CUPS (450G) SELF-RAISING FLOUR,
    PLUS EXTRA FOR DUSTING
½ TSP FINE SALT
80G UNSALTED BUTTER, CHILLED (SEE TIP)
¼ CUP (55G) CASTER SUGAR
250G FRESH DATES, PITTED, ROUGHLY CHOPPED
300ML BUTTERMILK
SALTED BUTTER OR JAM AND CREAM, TO SERVE

I was raised a country girl, but in the school holidays I used to stay with my Aunty Edna in Newcastle. She was one of nine siblings raised on an isolated farm and was the only girl apart from her twin sister, who died when they were just little cherubs. Aunty Edna practically raised those boys and my word could she bake. Some of the finest date scones I ever tasted came from her kitchen. These scones remind me of her and the impact that baking can have on the ones you love. **NADINE INGRAM**

date scones

MAKES 8

TIP

Take the butter out of the fridge to soften for 30 minutes before you begin so that you can rub it into the flour.

1 Preheat the oven to 170°C. Line a large baking tray with baking paper.

2 Sift the flour and salt together into a bowl, then rub in the butter using your fingertips until the mixture looks like fine breadcrumbs, with no lumps remaining. Add the sugar and chopped dates and toss them through roughly, using your hands.

3 Trickle half the buttermilk over the flour and, with a gentle touch, work it through using your fingertips. Pour the remaining buttermilk into the dough, incorporating it to mould the dough into a ball.

4 Tip the dough out onto a lightly floured surface and use the palms of your hands to flatten it to a 3cm thick round. Sprinkle a little more flour on top, then cut the scones out using a round cutter or an upturned glass. Dip the cutter into the flour before cutting each scone – this will stop the scone from sticking and will encourage a better rise.

5 Space the scones out on the tray, leaving 4cm between each one. Bake for 20 minutes, until golden brown.

6 Serve the scones with a slather of salted butter or copious amounts of jam and thick cream.

6 EGG WHITES, AT ROOM TEMPERATURE

1½ CUPS (330G) CASTER SUGAR

1 TABLESPOON CORNFLOUR

2 TEASPOONS WHITE VINEGAR

250G PUNNET STRAWBERRIES, HALVED

2 OR 3 FRESH PASSIONFRUIT

FRESH MINT LEAVES OR STRAWBERRY FLOWERS
FROM THE GARDEN, TO DECORATE

CHANTILLY CREAM

1½ CUPS (375ML) THICKENED CREAM

⅓ CUP (40G) ICING SUGAR, SIFTED

1 TEASPOON ORGANIC VANILLA BEAN PASTE

As a child I lived on 5 acres on the outskirts of Sydney in a working-class family with a couple of dairy cows, a few sheep, chickens and a vegie patch. We only had dessert on special occasions, and the choice was simple: pavlova, bread-and-butter pudding or ice-cream. All three were made with fresh eggs and cream skimmed from the milk bucket. **DARLENE ALLSTON**

classic pavlova with chantilly cream

SERVES 8–10

1 Place the top rack in the centre of the oven. Preheat the oven to 140°C. Draw a 20cm circle on a sheet of baking paper and place on a large greased baking tray, with the marked side down.

2 Beat the egg whites in the bowl of an electric mixer until soft peaks form. Gradually add the sugar, a tablespoon at a time, beating well after each addition. Once the sugar is dissolved, beat for 5 minutes, until thick and glossy.

3 Using a large metal spoon, quickly fold in the cornflour and vinegar. Spoon the mixture into the middle of the tray, keep the mixture piled high inside the circle, and make a slight indent in the centre.

4 Bake the pavlova on the middle rack of the oven for 1 hour, until it forms a thick crust. At this stage the crust should be pale/off-white in colour. If the pavlova begins to colour too quickly, reduce the temperature.

5 Reduce the oven to 120°C. Bake the pavlova for 30–45 minutes, until firm in the centre and the crust is dry to touch. Leave to cool in the oven with the door slightly ajar for 2 hours.

6 To make the chantilly cream, place the cream, icing sugar and vanilla into a mixing bowl. Using an electric mixer, beat until thickened.

7 To serve, spread the cream in the centre of the cooled pavlova. Top with the strawberries and passionfruit pulp. Decorate with mint leaves or strawberry flowers.

STEVE WEBBER

BEEKEEPER, BINGARA, NSW

A jar of honey plonked on the breakfast table along with a slab of butter and a pile of hot toast is part of the morning ritual for millions of Australians. But do we realise what goes into creating that tub of liquid gold, or how vital bees are to our ecosystem? Given that 75 per cent of the world's crops rely on pollination, apiarists such as Steve Webber are doing farming work that's critical to our food supply.

Steve, who lives with his wife Suzy and young daughter Harriett in Bingara, in NSW's Northern Rivers region, has been beekeeping for 10 years. He loved the idea "as a young bloke", but his parents suggested he try other careers first – and stints in radio and video production followed. "They wanted me to use my brain a bit more, which is ironic as there's a fair bit of brain work with beekeeping," he laughs.

Eventually, Steve tired of the work he was doing and was "a bit lost". He and Suzy had a small 40-acre farm, and his wife suggested he try beekeeping because he had the knowledge from his father, who was also an apiarist. Steve started out with just 20 hives; now he has 500, mostly on private property. "I like the thought of them being safe on farms and providing pollinating services where needed," he explains. "I follow the different flowering cycles of Australia's unique eucalypt species by trucking the bees to the trees. I really enjoy that part of it and the research I do. I've become a bit of a backyard botanist."

Moving bees is just one part of the heavy lifting: Steve also regularly checks his hives for disease, monitors pollen supplies and assesses how each queen bee is performing. Then there's extracting the honey – in a good year, Steve can produce 35 to 40 tonnes. "It's one of the very few low-impact harvests, as far as food crops go, and harvesting a tank of pure Australian honey, something you know people love, is really satisfying."

However, like so many Australian farming communities, Bingara is in the grip of drought and Steve sees firsthand how the dry conditions are affecting the farms he uses. "Drought just picks away at you. We're all doing it tough; my beekeeper mates have helped me out when I've needed it and I'll repay the favour when I can. It's good to talk to other farmers, I find. There's always someone doing it tougher than you. Aussies who support the croppers, the farmers, the beekeepers – they're keeping little towns and businesses ticking over."

Steve, who recently landed a contract to supply Beechworth Honey, says his priority is to keep his bees healthy, scout out other prospective farms and trees and just keep pushing on. "As a farmer, you just have to get up in the morning and keep going. Don't listen to weather reports. Just have hope in Mother Nature and wait for the sound of the bloody rain on the roof again. It'll come when it comes."

honey ginger snaps

MAKES 12–16

150G BUTTER

¼ CUP (90G) HONEY

1½ CUPS (225G) PLAIN FLOUR

1 TEASPOON BAKING POWDER

3 TEASPOONS GROUND GINGER

½ TEASPOON GROUND CINNAMON

½ TEASPOON GROUND NUTMEG

2 TABLESPOONS THINLY SLICED
   CRYSTALLISED GINGER

1 TABLESPOON RAW SUGAR

1   Preheat the oven to 180°C. Line three baking trays with baking paper.

2   Combine the butter and honey in a saucepan over low heat. Stir until the butter melts and the mixture begins to bubble. Remove the pan from the heat.

3   Sift the flour, baking powder and spices together, then stir into the honey mixture until smooth.

4   Roll tablespoons of the mixture into balls and place on the trays, leaving room for the biscuits to spread. Using your thumb, make an indent in the centre of each biscuit. Top each with a sliver of crystallised ginger and a sprinkle of raw sugar. Bake for 10 minutes, until golden. Cool the honey snaps on the trays.

3 EGGS

½ CUP (110G) CASTER SUGAR

150ML POURING CREAM

½ CUP (125ML) STRAINED FRESH LEMON JUICE

5 FINGER LIMES, TO SERVE

ICING SUGAR, FOR DUSTING (OPTIONAL)

THICK CREAM, TO SERVE

SWEET SHORTCRUST PASTRY

1½ CUPS (225G) PLAIN FLOUR, PLUS EXTRA
    FOR DUSTING

¼ CUP (30G) ICING SUGAR, SIFTED

¼ TEASPOON SALT

150G CHILLED BUTTER, CHOPPED

¼ CUP (60ML) ICED WATER

I grow and market finger limes for myself and a group of eight growers all over the country. We supply iconic Australian restaurants, distilleries and breweries, and export into Asia. I love everything about farming – I like to grow things and I like to see the results. **SHERYL RENNIE**

lemon tart with finger lime pearls

SERVES 8

1 To make the pastry, combine the flour, icing sugar and salt in a food processor. Add the butter and process until the mixture resembles fine breadcrumbs. Add the water and pulse until the mixture starts to come together.

2 Turn the pastry onto the bench and bring it together. Lightly knead with your fingertips for about 10 seconds. Shape the pastry into a disc, wrap in plastic wrap and place in the fridge for 20 minutes to rest.

3 Preheat the oven to 200°C. Gently flatten the pastry on a lightly floured surface with the palm of your hand. Roll out until 3mm thick. Transfer to a 23cm loose-based tart tin, pressing it into the join and the side. Roll the rolling pin over the top of the tin to trim any excess pastry.

4 Place the tin on a baking tray and prick the pastry base all over with a fork. Line the pastry with baking paper and fill with baking weights or dried beans. Bake for 20 minutes, remove the weights and paper and bake for a further 10 minutes, until the pastry base looks dry.

5 Meanwhile, whisk the eggs, caster sugar, cream and lemon juice in a bowl. Strain the mixture into a jug and pour into the hot pastry case while it is still on the oven rack.

6 Reduce the oven to 160°C. Bake the tart for 20–25 minutes, until the filling has just set in the centre but still wobbles slightly. Allow the tart to cool in the tin.

7 Decorate the cooled tart with finger lime pearls. Dust with icing sugar, if desired, and serve in wedges with the cream.

This recipe really came about from driving around the Byron hinterland. Mags and I had just made a sea change, moving away from the city to the country to join the new Three Blue Ducks adventure. Our first glimpse of what was to come was from driving around and discovering the honesty boxes at the driveways of the farms. Little sheds on the side of the road with honey, pumpkins, herbs, leafy greens, eggs laid that day and unpasteurised, unhomogenised milk straight from the dairy cows just metres away. Blown away with what was growing on our doorstep, we had found our new home.

This cake embraces all the ingredients we collected on the drive that first day – local honey, ricotta made from fresh milk infused with herbs, pasture-raised eggs and some citrus and macadamias, all grown by the amazing producers from the Byron hinterland. **DARREN ROBERTSON**

lemon, macadamia, thyme & ricotta cake

SERVES 6

200G UNSALTED BUTTER, SOFTENED, CHOPPED

⅔ CUP (150G) CASTER SUGAR

3 EGGS

250G RICOTTA

110G FINE POLENTA

30G HONEY, WARMED

GRATED ZEST OF 1 LEMON

JUICE OF 2 LEMONS

2 TEASPOONS BAKING POWDER

1 TEASPOON SEA SALT

1 SPRIG THYME

2 TABLESPOONS CHOPPED MACADAMIAS

1 Preheat oven to 160°C. Grease and line a 23cm x 13cm loaf tin.

2 Put the butter and caster sugar in a food processor. Process until the mixture is pale. Add the eggs, one at a time, processing until combined. Transfer to a large bowl.

3 Fold in the ricotta, polenta, honey, lemon zest, lemon juice, baking powder and salt. Pour into the tin. Poke six or seven little pieces of thyme into the top of the batter. Scatter the nuts over the top, pressing lightly.

4 Bake for 40–60 minutes, until the cake is golden brown and a skewer inserted in the centre comes out clean. Serve with berries, ricotta and a drizzle of honey.

250G SALTED BUTTER, CUBED, AT ROOM
    TEMPERATURE
1 CUP (125G) ICING SUGAR MIXTURE, SIFTED
1½ TEASPOONS VANILLA EXTRACT OR ESSENCE
1⅔ CUPS (250G) PLAIN FLOUR
½ CUP (60G) CORNFLOUR

ORANGE BUTTERCREAM FILLING
60G SALTED BUTTER, AT ROOM TEMPERATURE
GRATED ZEST OF 1 ORANGE
1 CUP (125G) ICING SUGAR MIXTURE, SIFTED

I grew up with these perennial favourites. Mum called her version 'radio biscuits' and she used custard powder instead of cornflour. They came from a dog-eared, well-loved Country Women's Association cookbook that she and I used a lot. I've used an orange buttercream filling for a citrus tang, but it's just as good flavoured with coffee, lemon or passionfruit. **ANNEKA MANNING**

melting moments

MAKES 18

1 Preheat the oven to 160°C. Line two large baking trays with baking paper.
2 Using an electric mixer, beat the butter, icing sugar and vanilla until pale and creamy. Sift the flour and cornflour over the butter mixture and beat on low speed until just combined and a soft dough forms.
3 Using lightly floured hands, roll heaped teaspoons of the mixture into balls. Place on the trays, about 5cm apart. Dip a fork in flour and use it to flatten the balls to 1cm thick and 4cm in diameter.
4 Bake the biscuits for 16–18 minutes, swapping the trays after 8 minutes, until pale golden and cooked through. Cool on the trays.
5 To make the filling, beat the butter and orange zest with an electric mixer until pale and creamy. Add the icing sugar and beat on low speed until combined. Increase the speed to high and beat until the buttercream is well combined and smooth.
6 Spread a little of the buttercream on the base of half the cooled biscuits and sandwich with another biscuit. Store the biscuits in an airtight jar or container in a cool place (not the fridge) for up to 4 days.

250G DARK CHOCOLATE, CHOPPED

250G BUTTER, CHOPPED

2½ CUPS (550G) CASTER SUGAR

1 TEASPOON VANILLA ESSENCE

5 EGGS, LIGHTLY BEATEN

⅓ CUP (50G) SELF-RAISING FLOUR

⅔ CUP (100G) PLAIN FLOUR

¼ CUP (30G) COCOA POWDER,
    PLUS EXTRA TO SERVE

¼ CUP (30G) DRINKING CHOCOLATE POWDER

CHOPPED CHOCOLATE, NUTS
    OR RASPBERRIES (OPTIONAL)

300ML THICKENED CREAM, WHIPPED

150G FRESH RASPBERRIES

My sister's beautiful gooey brownie is the BEST way to make friends. It's her favourite thing to take to a barbecue, a first day of work, on a long bus trip… you name it. She will whip out this brownie wherever she is and instantly have 15 new friends licking their fingers with joy. **ODETTE BARRY**

chocolate brownie

MAKES 15

1 Preheat the oven to 160°C. Grease and line a 28 cm x 18cm slice tin with baking paper, allowing the long edges to overhang the sides.

2 Place the chocolate and butter in a large heatproof bowl over a saucepan of simmering water, ensuring the water doesn't touch the bowl. Stir until melted and smooth.

3 Remove the bowl from the pan. Stir in the sugar and vanilla, then gradually add the egg, stirring until well combined. Sift the flours, cocoa powder and drinking chocolate over the top. Stir to combine.

4 Stir in the extra chocolate, nuts or raspberries, if using. Pour the batter into the tin. Bake for 45 minutes, until crisp on top but still moist in the middle. Cool completely in the tin.

5 Cut the cooled brownie into pieces. Serve with some whipped cream, raspberries and cocoa, if desired.

My family have lived on the land in north-east Victoria for four generations, farming sheep, cattle and wheat. I have fond memories of staying at my grandparents' farm. My nan, Gladys Wood, taught me how to cook on her wood stove. Her sponge cake is so famous it was even published in the *Australian Women's Weekly*!

Whether it was a Sunday roast, a cake for afternoon tea or baking for the shearers, there was always a great lesson to be learned in Nan's kitchen. She took great pride in providing morning tea (smoko), lunch and afternoon tea for the team of shearers who worked on the farm. The shearers ran to a stringent timetable so their meals had to be prepared strictly on time and needed to be hearty to sustain them throughout the day. I learned that country cooking is all about using fresh, paddock-to-plate ingredients and simple cooking techniques to create wholesome and delicious food. **CATHIE LONNIE**

feather-light sponge cake

SERVES 8–10

4 EGGS

¾ CUP (165G) CASTER SUGAR

¾ CUP (90G) WHEATEN CORNFLOUR

2 TABLESPOONS CUSTARD POWDER

1 TEASPOON CREAM OF TARTAR

½ TEASPOON BICARBONATE
  OF SODA

⅓ CUP (110G) RASPBERRY JAM

300ML THICKENED CREAM, WHIPPED

ICING SUGAR, FOR DUSTING

1 Preheat the oven to 180°C. Grease and flour two deep 20cm round cake tins.

2 Beat the eggs and caster sugar in a small bowl with an electric mixer for about 8 minutes, until thick, creamy and doubled in volume. Transfer to a large bowl. Gently fold in the triple-sifted dry ingredients.

3 Divide the batter evenly between the tins and bake for 20 minutes. Immediately turn the sponges out onto a wire rack lined with baking paper to cool.

4 Sandwich the sponges with jam and cream. Serve dusted with icing sugar.

1 CUP (170G) RAISINS

1 CUP (140G) CURRANTS

1 CUP (170G) SULTANAS

⅔ CUP (50G) MIXED PEEL

¾ CUP (100G) DRIED CRANBERRIES

½ CUP (125ML) SHERRY

2 TABLESPOONS MAPLE SYRUP

125G BUTTER, CHOPPED

1 CUP (220G) FIRMLY PACKED BROWN SUGAR

1 TEASPOON BICARBONATE OF SODA

1 TABLESPOON BOILING WATER

1 CUP (150G) PLAIN FLOUR

1 CUP (150G) SELF-RAISING FLOUR

½ TEASPOON GROUND CINNAMON

¼ TEASPOON EACH GROUND ALLSPICE,
   NUTMEG, CLOVES AND GINGER

2 EGGS, LIGHTLY BEATEN

1 TEASPOON VANILLA EXTRACT

¼ CUP (40G) BLANCHED ALMONDS

I grew up in a family of active girls who loved galloping around on ponies. I loved packing up the old Ford, with the horse float loaded up, and heading off to a horse event. There was nothing better than sitting in the front seat with Mum on a cold day, defrosting my fingers after a cross country event with a cup of tea and a chunk of her boiled fruit cake. **EMMA DEAN**

boiled fruit cake

SERVES 20

1 Combine the dried fruit, sherry and 1 cup (250ml) water in a large saucepan. Bring to the boil over medium heat. Reduce the heat to a simmer. Add the maple syrup, butter and brown sugar. Stir until the sugar is dissolved and the butter is melted. Remove the pan from the heat.

2 Combine the bicarbonate of soda and boiling water in a small bowl and stir quickly. Pour into the fruit mixture. Transfer to a large heatproof bowl and set aside to cool for 30 minutes.

3 Preheat the oven to 180°C. Lightly grease a 6cm deep, 20cm round cake tin and line with baking paper.

4 Put the flours and spices in a large bowl and mix together with a fork.

5 Stir the eggs and vanilla into the cooled fruit mixture, then stir in the dry ingredients. Pour the batter into the tin and level the surface. Top with the almonds.

6 Bake for 1¼ hours, then check the cake. If it is browning too quickly, turn the oven down slightly or cover with foil. Bake for a further 20–25 minutes, until the cake is firm to touch in the centre. Cool completely in the tin.

I grew up in Mudgee in central west NSW. Weekends were spent helping my mother make jams out of the boxes of goodies that friends brought her from their abundant gardens.

Love and family brought me to the Barossa Valley and gave me the opportunity to grow my preserve business, Lucy's Foods. I love my weekly trips to the local farmers' markets to discover what's on offer, and to provide me with fresh inspiration. There is nothing I love more than a drive to the Adelaide Hills or one of my local Barossa orchards to visit the growers who live and work there, and collect my fruit straight from the source. **LUCY LEWIS**

fig, pistachio & yoghurt cake

SERVES 12

¾ CUP (165G) FIRMLY PACKED BROWN SUGAR

200G UNSALTED BUTTER, CHOPPED

12 FRESH FIGS, HALVED

150G UNSALTED PISTACHIO KERNELS

1¼ CUPS (185G) SELF-RAISING FLOUR

1¼ CUPS (275G) CASTER SUGAR

3 EGGS

125G PLAIN YOGHURT

CREAM OR ICE-CREAM, TO SERVE

1 Preheat the oven to 160°C. Grease and line a 20cm springform cake tin.

2 Stir the brown sugar and 50g of the butter in a saucepan over low heat until smooth. Pour into the tin. Arrange two-thirds of the figs, cut-side down, on top.

3 Put the pistachios in a food processor and pulse until chopped. Add the remaining butter, flour and caster sugar and pulse for 20 seconds, until the mixture resembles breadcrumbs. Add the combined eggs and yoghurt and pulse until just combined.

4 Spoon the batter over the figs and smooth the surface. Bake for 1½ hours, until a skewer comes out clean when inserted into the cake. Leave in the tin for 5 minutes before inverting the cake onto a plate. Arrange the remaining figs on top of the cake. Serve warm with cream or ice-cream.

GILLIAN LEEDS

CATTLE FARMER, JERILDERIE, NSW

G illian Leeds has spent most of her life on the land – and wouldn't have it any other way. Growing up on her family property called Broome, in Jerilderie, New South Wales, Gillian spent a decade away as a young woman, returning in 1976 as a widow with three young children. Her widowed mother and a business partner were managing the 31-year-old shorthorn stud.

Gillian took on the shorthorns and in 1982 entered the Dubbo Show at the urging of a friend. As her flighty young bull was being broken in, unfortunately the trainer died, leaving Gillian to complete the job and get to the show four hours up the Newell Highway. A young man led the bull for her and when the beast won its class, he turned to Gillian. "Put your liptstick on," he said. "We're gonna win this!"

The young bull won Grand Champion. Gillian was the first woman to win at Dubbo, and the only woman breeder at the time. She persevered and years later showed more Grand Champion bulls and a cow.

"The idea is to breed moderate frame with everything in place: legs, temperament, doing ability," says Gillian. "There's a lot to breeding. You choose bulls based on marbling, nice EMA, and a big factor is calving ease."

During the 2000 drought, Broome cattle were trucked to areas that were not in drought: South Australia, Victoria, Queensland and other parts of New South Wales. Some of the couple of hundred cows were moved about eight times. Some heifers were lost to cattle rustlers. By 2010, with still no rain, the Broome Shorthorn stud of 320 cows, heifers and many calves was dispersed. During the on-farm sale, Gillian threw her hand up and bought back a couple of cows selling too cheap. One is still a Broome breeding heifer.

As her lifetime's work disappeared in trucks out the front gate, Gillian considered the hard day. It had been a completely financial decision.

Eight shorthorn heifers that had bolted up the road before the sale, together with the unsellable ones that had mastitis or were too thin, one that was blind and one that kept absconding, were used to rebuild a herd, which is now 50 cows. Leeds Shorthorns took out another grand champion bull at Dubbo in 2015.

The current drought has been so widespread that it's left nowhere suitable for Gillian to agist her cattle again. She will sell all the steers, but some farmers have sold all their stock. She's pragmatic about her decision.

"We haven't had any decent rain for almost a year now," she says. "You have to look after the country during drought, which is why I'm culling my stock again, only hanging onto our breeders. I love the land. I'm lucky here because I live in nature and it's a wonderful way to bring up free and happy children. I find housework harder than going out and drenching cattle."

GILLIAN LEEDS'S

my mother's cheesecake

SERVES 6–8

180G PLAIN SWEET BISCUITS (ARNOTT'S NICE
 OR MILK ARROWROOT), CRUSHED
125G BUTTER, MELTED AND COOLED
SQUEEZE OF FRESH LEMON JUICE
250G BLOCK CREAM CHEESE, AT ROOM
 TEMPERATURE
395G CAN SWEETENED CONDENSED MILK
½ CUP (125ML) FRESH LEMON JUICE
SEASONAL FRUIT, SUCH AS NECTARINES
 AND PASSIONFRUIT, TO DECORATE

1 Lightly grease a 20cm pie plate or invert the
   base of a 20cm springform cake tin and line
   with baking paper. Place the crushed biscuits
   in a bowl with the butter and lemon juice.
   Mix until well combined.

2 Press the crumbs into the base of the pie
   plate or tin, pressing in firmly with the base
   of a glass. Chill the base while you prepare
   the filling.

3 Place the cream cheese in the bowl of an
   electric mixer and beat until smooth. Add
   the condensed milk and beat until smooth.
   Add the lemon juice. Beat until combined.

4 Pour the filling over the base and level the
   surface. Chill for 4 hours, until firm.

5 Serve the cheesecake with seasonal fruits.

KOOLIE

'm Gem. You won't need to call me because I'll either be on the back of the work vehicle before you've opened the garden gate, or standing by your side. It's unlikely I'll ride all the way with you because I love to run. Gillian treats me like a human and I can't tell you how lucky I am to have fallen into her hands. After George the Kelpie passed away, she was heartbroken and friends delivered me to her door. She already knew my type, the Koolie, because her family had bred us intermittently for generations. She knew I was a gem and she named me that.

I am the rising star of working dogs. We've been in Australia about the same time as my rockstar cousins, the kelpies and the border collies, since the early 1800s. Unlike them, nobody got around to keeping breeding records and so we were never registered as an independent breed. It takes seven generations to do that, but we're now off and running and running and running. In fact, I've got the kelpie running from next door too. He comes in the night, crossing the paddocks and a deep creek, for our tete-a-tetes. We're a strong pair and our pups are in high demand. Gillian sells them for around $400 as working dogs, but the ace up my sleeve is the spotty pups. They're so unusual that an urban buyer will pay up to $1000. I'm eight years old now and I've had 29 pups, with only two remaining at home.

We are tough, loyal dogs, known for our high energy, herding instinct and kind disposition. If not working, we can be loyal and kind companion dogs. And we love kids! We come in all the usual colours and variations of black, tan and white, but a genetic difference is our blue eyes. If you breed me with another spotty koolie, there is a one-fifth chance that I'll throw a white pup with two blue eyes. That means vision and hearing impairments and we avoid that at all costs, so please always find me a solid-coloured mate.

When I'm relaxed my ears fold a little from the top, but when I'm alert, they are straight and rigid, like when the cattle are on the move or there is a snake lurking. Because we live on the creek we have a few extra fowl hanging around and I like to work every day so once we've fed all the cattle, I have a go at the stupid ducks. I sneak up behind them and stalk, singling out the hen and cutting her from the drakes. It keeps us all on our toes.

In the yards I'll stalk the cattle, waiting for instruction from Gillian but, really, I know what to do. I'll stare those cattle down and keep them in their place until I'm told to move them on. Some individual training early on saved me getting bad habits from my close mates in the yards. We worked through Sit, Go Back, Cover Over, and Way Back, which means to go right around the mob. Most days in our downtime I will go and eyeball the cattle just to keep my hand in.

I am polite to the other humans who live on the farm, but I'll not take orders from them. My place is with my boss and I won't be moved. I expect to live until I'm 15 years old, but the way Gillian treats me I will probably live beyond that – and a hell of a lot longer than the ducks.

450G RHUBARB STALKS, TRIMMED

300G FRESH OR FROZEN RASPBERRIES

250G CASTER SUGAR

40G PLAIN FLOUR

1 TEASPOON FINELY GRATED LEMON ZEST

1 TEASPOON ROSEWATER

1 TABLESPOON GRANULATED SUGAR

DOUBLE CREAM, TO SERVE

SHORTCRUST PASTRY

240G PLAIN FLOUR, PLUS EXTRA FOR DUSTING

½ TEASPOON SALT

180G CHILLED BUTTER, COARSELY CHOPPED

70ML ICED WATER

I grew up on Sydney's northern beaches when much of the hinterland behind Mona Vale was full of market gardens. Every week my mum would visit one of the farms to buy eggs and vegies. I loved going with her, as the farmer and his wife would welcome us with open arms. I realise how fortunate I was to grow up understanding where my food came from. **BELINDA JEFFERY**

rhubarb & raspberry crostata

SERVES 8–10

1   To make the pastry, whisk the flour and salt in a bowl to combine. Tip onto a work surface and scatter the chunks of butter over the top. Using your fingertips, rub in the butter to resemble coarse breadcrumbs. Make a well in the centre and pour in the iced water. Using a pastry scraper in a mixing and chopping motion, combine into a streaky dough, making sure not to overwork the dough.

2   Use the heel of your hand to knead the dough (you should be able to see streaks of butter in the pastry). Gently work into a disc, then divide into four portions and wrap each portion in plastic wrap. Refrigerate for 40 minutes, until the pastry is firm but supple enough to roll out.

3   Meanwhile, slice the rhubarb into 4–5 cm lengths and put in a large bowl with the raspberries (if using frozen raspberries, there is no need to thaw them), caster sugar, flour, lemon zest and rosewater, and gently mix with your hands to combine.

4   Preheat the oven to 200°C. Line a large baking tray with baking paper. On a lightly floured surface, roll out each pastry disc into a thin round. Spread the fruit mixture over the pastry rounds, leaving a border of about 4cm. Fold the excess pastry over the fruit, pleating and pressing gently to seal it and form a border. Sprinkle the granulated sugar over the top.

5   Bake for 20–30 minutes, until the pastry is crisp and deep golden brown. Cool on the tray for 40 minutes so the filling firms up. Serve with double cream, if desired.

I'm a worry farmer. There's always something going on – cows calving, calves weaning, not enough water, too much water, animals dying. My daughter tells me, "You're gonna have live ones and your gonna have dead ones. You can't keep 'em all." It's that simple, I suppose, but it's never easy. **DIDIE GRIFFIN**

passionfruit tarts

MAKES 18

TIP

Use smaller tartlet cases to make 24 bite-sized tarts.

300ML THICKENED CREAM

395G CAN SWEETENED CONDENSED MILK

¼ CUP (60ML) FRESH LEMON JUICE

½ CUP (125ML) FRESH PASSIONFRUIT PULP
   (ABOUT 4 PASSIONFRUIT)

18 X 8CM SHORTCRUST PASTRY TARTLET CASES

EXTRA PASSIONFRUIT, TO SERVE (OPTIONAL)

1   Whip the cream until stiff peaks form. Fold in the condensed milk, lemon juice and passionfruit pulp.

2   Spoon the passionfruit mixture into the tartlet cases. Refrigerate for 1 hour, until the mixture is firm.

3   Serve the chilled tarts topped with extra passionfruit pulp, if using.

125G BUTTER, MELTED AND COOLED,
PLUS EXTRA FOR GREASING

400G TILBA REAL DAIRY CREAM CHEESE,
SOFTENED

450G RICOTTA

1½ CUPS (330G) CASTER SUGAR

4 LARGE EGGS

¼ CUP (35G) PLAIN FLOUR

¼ CUP (30G) CORNFLOUR

1 TABLESPOON LEMON JUICE

1 TABLESPOON VANILLA BEAN PASTE

490G (2 CUPS) SOUR CREAM

BERRY COMPOTE, TO SERVE (OPTIONAL)

TILBA REAL DAIRY DOUBLE CREAM, TO SERVE

I just love that whole process of nurturing something and turning it into food. I've always believed you are what you eat, and we want the milk that we produce on our farm in Tilba to be the very best it can be for the good health of everyone who buys it. **ERICA DIBDEN**

baked ricotta cheesecake

SERVES 10–12

TIP

The cheesecake will keep in an airtight container in the fridge for up to 4 days.

1 Preheat the oven to 160°C. Grease a 22cm springform cake tin with melted butter and line with baking paper. Tightly wrap the base and side of the pan with foil to prevent any water seeping in during baking.

2 Using an electric mixer, beat the softened cream cheese until smooth. Gradually beat in the ricotta until smooth. Gradually beat in the sugar over 1 minute, scraping down the side of the bowl when required. Once all the sugar is incorporated, beat for a further 30 seconds.

3 Add the eggs, one at a time, beating well after each addition. Beat in the sifted flour and cornflour, and the lemon juice and vanilla. Add the cooled melted butter and sour cream. Beat for 30 seconds, until well combined and smooth.

4 Pour the mixture into the cake tin. Place the tin in a roasting tin and pour in enough boiling water to reach halfway up the side of the cake tin. Bake the cheesecake for 60–70 minutes, until the centre is slightly soft and wobbles slightly when the tin is shaken. Remove the tin from the water bath and set aside on a wire rack to cool completely. Cover and place in the fridge overnight.

5 Serve the cheesecake with the berry compote, if using, and double cream.

125G UNSALTED BUTTER, CHOPPED

350G DARK COOKING CHOCOLATE,
FINELY CHOPPED

1¼ CUPS (130G) HAZELNUT MEAL

½ CUP (100G) BROWN SUGAR

⅓ CUP (40G) COCOA POWDER

5 EGGS, SEPARATED

2 TEASPOONS VANILLA EXTRACT

½ CUP (125ML) POURING CREAM

DOUBLE CREAM OR CRÈME FRAÎCHE, TO SERVE

HAZELNUT PRALINE

⅔ CUP (110G) HAZELNUTS, ROASTED, SKINNED

⅔ CUP (150G) CASTER SUGAR

Our family farm, 'Belwarra', is in the central west of NSW in a small town in the Cowra region called Woodstock. It's predominantly a beef and sheep farm, but we also have more than 2000 hazelnut trees. There is so much more to rural living than just farming – the strong sense of community and helping each other is what life is all about. **MICHELLE SOUTHAN**

flourless chocolate hazelnut cake

SERVES 8

1 Preheat the oven to 180°C. Grease a 22cm springform cake tin and line with baking paper.

2 Combine the butter and 250g of the chocolate in a small saucepan over low heat and stir until melted and smooth. Combine the hazelnut meal, brown sugar and cocoa in a large bowl. Add the chocolate mixture, egg yolks and vanilla. Stir until well combined.

3 Using an electric mixer, beat the egg whites in a clean, dry bowl until firm peaks form. Use a large metal spoon to fold the egg whites into the chocolate mixture in three batches until just combined. Spoon into the cake tin and smooth the surface. Bake for 40 minutes, until a skewer inserted into the centre comes out clean. Leave in the tin for 15 minutes before transferring to a wire rack to cool.

4 To make the praline, spread the roasted hazelnuts over a baking tray lined with baking paper. Combine the caster sugar and ⅓ cup (80ml) water in a small saucepan over low heat. Cook, stirring, for 3 minutes, until the sugar has dissolved. Increase the heat to high and bring to the boil. Cook, brushing down the side of the pan with a wet pastry brush, for 3–5 minutes, until golden. Pour the hot syrup over the hazelnuts. Set aside for 5 minutes to firm up, then break into shards.

5 Combine the cream and remaining 100g of chocolate in a small saucepan over medium-low heat. Cook, stirring, for 3 minutes, until the mixture is smooth.

6 Top the cake with the double cream, drizzle with the chocolate sauce and scatter with the hazelnut praline.

COURTNEY YOUNG & IAN CONGDON

FLOUR MILLER, BERRIGAN, NSW

S ometimes a successful rural business is less about growing things, but instead about taking advantage of what the community grows and turning it into something special. This is the story of Courtney Young and her partner Ian Congdon. The couple moved to Berrigan in southern NSW in 2016. Back on the family farm they established a small flour milling business, producing wholegrain, stoneground flour. The flour is milled fresh to order, from grains that Ian and Courtney sow with his family. Woodstock flour is the result.

Ian's parents, Bob and Jenny Congdon, grow livestock at Woodstock as well as wheat, rye and oats. Ian is the fourth generation to work the beautiful 2000-acre property. With an existing 20-year organic certification on the land, Courtney and Ian began growing spelt and an ancient grain named khorasan. In 2018 they began trialling a few heritage wheat varieties.

Courtney's dedication is rooted in the belief that our landscapes should be regenerated and re-peopled. As an environmentalist, she doesn't believe in locking up land for conservation, but rather living in and caring for it so it can continue to feed and support us.

With a young daughter to care for, her time is divided between the mill house and the occasional foray into the sheep yards. She loves the unpredictability and craziness that stock work can bring, but nothing compares to the early morning routine of the mill house.

Every second week it takes five full days to collect grain from the silos then mill, bag up and package the flour. Flour deliveries are done in person to the bakers in Melbourne and the three-hour return journey is sweetened by the taste of the gifted pastries.

"We're hopeful that the drought will break soon," says Courtney. "My parents-in-law have lived through this all before and their experience and support is invaluable. Ian and I are lucky we can value-add to our grain and set our own prices to help get us through."

Grains are considered the last frontier of the local food movement and Courtney and Ian wanted to see grains celebrated for their regionality and flavour rather than simply viewed as a commodity. They also saw flour milling as a way to get involved in the family farm and ensure its viability well into the future. It's been a massive learning curve because there aren't many small-scale stone millers in Australia.

This year has been tough and another bad year will see no grain, no flour and no fodder for the sheep. Again, flexibility helps. Courtney supplements their income working one day per week for the local Landcare and Ian occasionally labours for neighbours.

However, despite these constant drought concerns, Courtney finds her fellow farmers painfully optimistic. Their faith and innovation has taught her to look at life with a smile. They always manage to have a laugh, even in the face of adversity – and she has learnt that many things can be fixed with blue baling twine or a bit of fencing wire!

125G BUTTER, MELTED AND COOLED,
    PLUS EXTRA FOR GREASING
1 LARGE (ABOUT 200G) ROYAL GALA,
    PINK LADY OR GOLDEN DELICIOUS APPLE
1 TABLESPOON LEMON JUICE
1 TABLESPOON CASTER SUGAR
1½ CUPS (240G) WHOLEGRAIN,
    STONEGROUND, FRESH SPELT FLOUR
2 TEASPOONS BAKING POWDER
1 CUP (220G) RAW SUGAR
2 EGGS, AT ROOM TEMPERATURE
½ CUP (125ML) MILK
1 TEASPOON VANILLA EXTRACT

RICOTTA FILLING

250G FRESH RICOTTA, DRAINED
GRATED ZEST OF 1 LEMON
1 TABLESPOON CASTER SUGAR
2 EGG YOLKS

CRUMBLE TOPPING

½ CUP (80G) WHOLEGRAIN, STONEGROUND,
    FRESH SPELT FLOUR
50G CHILLED BUTTER, CHOPPED
½ CUP (110G) FIRMLY PACKED BROWN SUGAR

COURTNEY YOUNG'S

spelt, apple & ricotta cake

SERVES 8

1 Preheat the oven to 160°C. Grease a 20cm springform cake tin with melted butter and line the base with baking paper.

2 To make the ricotta filling, mix the ricotta, lemon zest, caster sugar and egg yolks in a bowl until well combined. Cover and place in the fridge.

3 To make the crumble topping, rub the spelt flour and butter together with your fingertips until it resembles coarse breadcrumbs. Stir in the brown sugar. Place in the fridge.

4 Peel, core and quarter the apple. Cut into thin slices and toss in a bowl with the lemon juice and caster sugar until evenly combined.

5 Sift the spelt flour and baking powder into a large bowl. Stir in the raw sugar. Whisk together the melted butter, eggs, milk and vanilla. Pour into the dry ingredients. Mix until just combined.

6 Pour the batter into the cake tin. Drain the sliced apple and arrange on top of the batter. Spread the ricotta filling over the top to cover the apple, then sprinkle evenly with the crumble topping.

7 Bake the cake for 60–65 minutes, until it is golden and cooked through when tested with a skewer. Leave on a wire rack to cool. Serve with whipped cream.

SOFT BUTTER, FOR GREASING

¼ CUP (55G) CASTER SUGAR, PLUS
2 TABLESPOONS FOR COATING

200G GOOD-QUALITY DARK CHOCOLATE,
CHOPPED (NO MORE THAN 50%
COCOA BUTTER)

50G BUTTER, CHOPPED

4 EGG YOLKS

7 EGG WHITES

SIFTED COCOA POWDER OR ICING SUGAR,
TO SERVE

VANILLA ICE-CREAM, TO SERVE

I am proud to have been on the Council of the Royal Agricultural Society of NSW since 1996 and subsequently to become the first female Vice President. I have a deep love for this organisation and its charter to promote agricultural excellence via exhibition, competition and education. We value our farmers, and the Fine Food competitions we inaugurated in 1998 always reflect the results of the climate on what our hard-working farmers produce.

   These soufflés use only a few simple ingredients, none of which are hard for people who live in the country to find, something which I think is always important. The recipe is foolproof, guaranteeing success to even a novice cook yet with spectacular results. It's my homage to farmers who, despite challenges, give us spectacular results. **LYNDEY MILAN**

chocolate soufflés

MAKES 6

1   Preheat the oven to 200°C. Brush six ½ cup (125ml) ovenproof dishes with butter. Place 2 tablespoons of the caster sugar in one of the dishes. Turn to coat the base and side, then tip the excess into the next dish. Repeat until all the dishes are coated. Place on a baking tray.

2   Combine the chocolate and butter in a small saucepan over very low heat, stirring until melted. Remove from the heat. Whisk in the egg yolks.

3   Beat the egg whites in a large bowl with an electric mixer until soft peaks form. Gradually add the caster sugar, beating until the mixture is thick and glossy.

4   Using a large balloon whisk, gently fold one-third of the egg white mixture into the chocolate mixture. Fold in the remaining egg white mixture.

5   Divide the batter among the prepared dishes. Smooth the tops with the back of a knife. Run your thumb and forefinger around the rims to release the mixture from the edges.

6   Bake for 12–15 minutes, until the soufflés are puffed. Dust with sifted cocoa or icing sugar and serve straight away with vanilla ice-cream.

My husband manages 50,000 acres, three properties, one of which we live on with our two daughters. As a manager, he planned ahead and sold what stock he could, but at the moment he spends each day doing 'meals on wheels' – feeding stock. Everything else has been put on hold and it is a fairly monotonous and mind-numbing task. **SALLY EMPRINGHAM**

lemonade scones

MAKES 12

3 CUPS (450G) PLAIN FLOUR,
    PLUS EXTRA FOR DUSTING
1 CUP (250ML) LEMONADE
1 CUP (250ML) THICKENED CREAM
1 EGG, LIGHTLY BEATEN
STRAWBERRY JAM AND WHIPPED CREAM,
    TO SERVE

1   Preheat the oven to 220°C.

2   Place the flour in a large bowl and make a well in the centre. Combine the lemonade and thickened cream in a jug. Pour into the dry ingredients. Using a knife, gently stir until the mixture forms a soft, sticky dough.

3   Turn the dough out onto a floured surface and press gently into a 3cm thick round. Cut out rounds using a 5cm cutter. Place on a baking tray lined with baking paper. Brush with the beaten egg.

4   Bake for 10–15 minutes, until the scones are golden. Place inside a tea towel to keep warm while you wait for the farmer to come home (their half an hour means 3 hours and they are never on time). Serve the scones with strawberry jam and whipped cream.

Fresh pikelets were cooked every morning for the week-long shearing season. Mum was a stickler for being punctual for the shearers. Most importantly, the pikelets had to be hot and smothered in melting butter. As a young teenager, I was in charge of the morning tea run. Making the perfect pikelets required good time management skills alongside this fail-proof recipe. **ROSLYN ANDERSON**

shearers' pikelets

MAKES 28

2 CUPS (300G) SELF-RAISING FLOUR

¼ TEASPOON BICARBONATE OF SODA

¼ CUP (55G) CASTER SUGAR

PINCH OF SALT

1 EGG

1½ CUPS (375ML) MILK

½ TEASPOON WHITE VINEGAR

20G BUTTER, MELTED

BUTTER, TO SERVE

1 Sift the flour and bicarbonate of soda into a large bowl. Add the sugar and salt.

2 Mix the egg, milk and vinegar in a small bowl. Pour into the dry ingredients and mix well. Set the batter aside for 30 minutes.

3 Heat a large heavy-based frying pan over medium–high heat and lightly grease with the melted butter. Drop dessertspoons of the batter into the pan. Cook until bubbles appear on the surface and the base is golden. Turn and cook on the other side until golden.

4 Spread the pikelets with butter while hot.

DAN WALKER

AGRI-TOURISM, LONGREACH, QLD

———

Most afternoons at sunset, Dan Walker can be found in a paddock at Camden Park Station, taking in the kaleidoscopic colours of the outback sky and the 360-degree views to Longreach, Ilfracombe and beyond. For the lucky tourists who join him, it's a rare opportunity to watch the sun sink beyond the horizon without a man-made piece of infrastructure in sight.

"The sunset is really special," he says. "At sunrise, you've got a big day ahead of you, but at sunset you can enjoy the day that was. The views we get are tremendous, not a cloud in the sky."

A fifth-generation farmer, Dan, known as Outback Dan, grew up mustering stock on his family's 18,000-acre Camden Park Station, which was bought by his grandfather in 1962. The property is still home to Dorper sheep, but these days Dan and his brother James have branched out into other ventures including a 55,000-panel solar farm, a financial planning tool for producers known as Agrihive, and Dan's passion, tourism.

Capitalising on Camden Park Station's stunning views and history – the property played host to Queen Elizabeth and Prince Philip in 1970 – Dan now hosts tours of the property, showing visitors its artesian springs, shearing sheds, cattle yards and homestead, complete with the oldest private ballroom in the outback.

Dan says that it's the people he meets on these tours that help him stay positive during tough times. "They really enjoy the stories and their support for me and my family is incredible," he says.

His family's connection to the land and the resilient, have-a-go attitude of local farmers are other sources of inspiration for Dan. "There's this feeling of the land being inside your blood. We feel like we're just custodians for the next generation," he says. "The men and women of the land are hardened by the weather. They're strongly resilient. You gotta go with it and not let it get you down too far."

For Dan, this means always creating a green environment around the home and embracing the larrikin spirit of the bush. Case in point: Dan and James have established the Outback Yacht Club, hosting regattas and social events around the property's artesian bore. "You've got to have a bit of the joke in you," he says.

Despite the challenges of life on the land, Dan wouldn't have it any other way. "It's a great place to bring up children. It teaches them independence and resilience. And I love the community. I couldn't picture being anywhere else."

DAN WALKER'S

never-fail chocolate cake

SERVES 8

TIP

To make a coffee cake, replace the cocoa with 1 tablespoon instant coffee, dissolved in 1 tablespoon boiling water. For a vanilla cake, omit the cocoa, increase the vanilla essence to 2 teaspoons and add an extra 2 tablespoons of flour.

1½ CUPS (225G) SELF-RAISING FLOUR

1¼ CUPS (275G) CASTER SUGAR

1 CUP (250ML) MILK

125G BUTTER, CHOPPED, AT ROOM
    TEMPERATURE

2 EGGS

2 TABLESPOONS COCOA POWDER

1 TEASPOON VANILLA ESSENCE

1 TEASPOON BAKING POWDER

CHOCOLATE ICING

1 CUP (125G) ICING SUGAR

2 TABLESPOONS COCOA POWDER

30G BUTTER, MELTED

2 TABLESPOONS MILK

1. Preheat the oven to 180°C. Grease a 20cm round cake tin and line with baking paper.

2. Using an electric mixer, beat the flour, caster sugar, milk, butter, eggs, cocoa, vanilla and baking powder in a large bowl on low speed for 1 minute, until combined. Increase the speed and beat for 4 minutes, until smooth and paler in colour.

3. Pour the batter into the cake tin. Bake for 55–60 minutes, until a skewer inserted into the centre comes out clean. Leave the cake in the tin for 10 minutes before turning out onto a wire rack to cool completely.

4. To make the icing, sift the icing sugar and cocoa into a bowl. Stir in the melted butter and enough of the milk to make a smooth, spreadable icing. Spread over the cake.

I make this every year for Christmas and cattlework. It was originally called apricot marshmallow roll. One of the contractors who musters for us would never eat any because he thought it had banana in it. Once he realised it was banana free, he changed his mind, but we've called it banana roll ever since. **WENDY SHEEHAN**

banana roll

MAKES 50 PIECES

250G MARIE BISCUITS

⅔ CUP (HALF A 395G CAN) SWEETENED
  CONDENSED MILK

125G BUTTER, CHOPPED

125G DRIED APRICOTS, FINELY CHOPPED

140G MARSHMALLOWS, FINELY CHOPPED

½ CUP (45G) DESICCATED OR
  SHREDDED COCONUT

1 Put the biscuits in a food processor and process until finely crushed.

2 Combine the condensed milk and butter in a saucepan. Stir over low heat until melted and smooth. Stir in the crushed biscuits, apricots and marshmallows.

3 Place two large sheets of baking paper on a clean work surface. Using wet hands, roll the mixture into two logs about 4cm thick. Place the coconut on a tray. Roll the logs in the coconut, then wrap in the baking paper and twist the ends to secure. Refrigerate until set.

4 Cut the logs into 1cm slices to serve.

1½ CUPS (140G) ROLLED OATS

1¼ CUPS (55G) RICE BUBBLES

1½ CUPS (130G) DESICCATED COCONUT

6 WEET-BIX, CRUSHED

1 CUP (165G) DRIED APRICOTS, CHOPPED

½ CUP (90G) SULTANAS

1¼ CUPS (230G) LIGHTLY PACKED BROWN SUGAR

¾ CUP (260G) HONEY

¾ CUP (200G) PEANUT BUTTER

180G BUTTER, CHOPPED

CHOCOLATE TOPPING

200G DARK COOKING CHOCOLATE, MELTED

30G BUTTER

We have a family property in outback Queensland, which is home to 2000 wool-growing merinos, 600 cows and us. This slice is a cattlework staple. We were involved in the NIRS (Near Infrared Reflectance Spectroscopy) trial, where we collected dung samples from the cattle herd every month, dried the collected dung in the oven and mailed it to Brisbane to be analysed for cattle health and nutrition. My niece was here at the time and said that the slice looked rather similar to the oven-dried samples. **WENDY SHEEHAN**

cow poo slice

MAKES 24 PIECES

1 Grease a 32cm x 22cm cake tin and line with baking paper, extending 2cm over the long sides.

2 Combine the rolled oats, rice bubbles, coconut, Weet-Bix and fruit in a large bowl.

3 Combine the brown sugar, honey, peanut butter and butter in a saucepan and stir over low heat until the sugar dissolves. Increase the heat and simmer, stirring constantly, for 5 minutes, until the mixture thickens slightly. Stir the honey into the dry ingredients until well combined. Press evenly into the tin and refrigerate for 3 hours, until set.

4 To make the topping, combine the chocolate with the butter, stirring until smooth. Drizzle over the slice. Return to the fridge until set. Lift the slice from the tin and cut into squares.

I grew up spending holidays at my Aunty Didie and Uncle Jeff's farm in Kempsey. We were allowed to run wild there and I have many wonderful memories of green paddocks stretching as far as the eye could see, side-splitting laughter and this feeling deep inside me that I'd found my happy place when I was there. **JODY VASSALLO**

condensed milk choc-chip cookies

MAKES 22

250G BUTTER, SOFTENED

½ CUP (110G) CASTER SUGAR

200ML SWEETENED CONDENSED MILK

2½ CUPS (375G) PLAIN FLOUR

3½ TEASPOONS BAKING POWDER

300G DARK CHOCOLATE, ROUGHLY CHOPPED

1 Preheat the oven to 150°C. Line two large baking trays with baking paper.

2 Using an electric mixer, beat the butter and sugar with the condensed milk until pale and creamy. Sift the flour and baking powder together over the butter mixture and mix until the dough almost comes together. Add the chocolate and stir until well combined.

3 Roll heaped tablespoons of the mixture into balls and place on the trays, allowing a little room for spreading. Flatten slightly with your fingertips or a fork. Bake for 9–12 minutes, until the biscuits are light golden. Leave on the trays for 5 minutes before transferring to a wire rack to cool.

HELEN ELIAS

CROP FARMER, CONDOBOLIN, NSW

For Helen Elias, rural life is all about family. She and her husband Peter have seven children and, while life was difficult and lonely in those early years on their farm, she says she feels blessed with the results of their hard work.

One of four brothers who headed west to make their way and learn the farming business, Peter took Helen and their two oldest children out to learn farming with the idea that they would make their fortune and return to Sydney.

"This farm came up and then, the family, the four brothers got together, had a bit of a meeting and decided that yeah, we're going to go farming. So we all agreed, packed up and left, thinking we're going to go away and do really well in a few years," Helen explains. "So we came, and when we arrived things didn't work out. The drought set in. And we just kept plodding along, thinking it's going to end, it's going to end. It was a pretty horrific start. Especially for me, more than anyone, because I got depression, and I thought, 'I've just got to leave this place, I can't stand it, I can't live here.' But I kept on trying and trying, and 41 years later we're still here. And yes, it was the best thing that could've happened to me."

While the farm originally had livestock, the family has moved it to cropping, particularly wheat and seed canola, which is at a premium because of its high quality. The farm has its ups and downs, weather depending, but it's been a success for the family.

Now 67 and looking back on her youthful self, Helen is glad she stuck it out. Her son Jared and his wife Lisa now live and work on the farm, while the others have moved on to successful city careers. She and Peter have 22 grandchildren.

"We were lucky enough to be here to have the time with our children on the land, and to be there to instil all those kinds of things in them without any distractions. And we've made some great friends, and as a family life, it's just been wonderful for us."

Born in Lebanon, Helen had grown up in a local Lebanese community where, she says, "everyone thought the same way, and we all did the same things".

"When we came out here I learned so much about life," she says. "I had post-natal depression twice, which taught me so much. It taught me to leave a lot of things that wouldn't be important alone, and to get on and focus on what was important. And to see the upside of things, to see the other side of life. Not to be judgemental, or angry about a lot of things."

Those early years also taught Helen pragmatism and resilience. "We had our first lot of rain a couple of days ago, which was an inch, the first we've had for 11 months. When we arrived, for the first 10 years, I think I would have been worried, and angry, and upset, and want to get out of here and turn my back on everything, but going through depression and going through those things has made me realise that what will be will be, we'll just keep on going, and we learned that everything does change."

LISA ELIAS'S

vanilla, coconut & mixed berry crumble

SERVES 6

750G STRAWBERRIES, HALVED

250G BLUEBERRIES

125G BLACKBERRIES

2 TEASPOONS VANILLA BEAN PASTE

140G PLAIN FLOUR, SIFTED

130G CASTER SUGAR

120G BUTTER, SOFTENED

70G SHREDDED COCONUT

VANILLA BEAN ICE-CREAM,
    TO SERVE

1   Preheat the oven to 180°C.

2   Combine the berries and vanilla bean paste
    in an 8 cup (2 litre) ovenproof dish.

3   Combine the flour and sugar in a large bowl.
    Using your fingertips, rub in the butter until
    fine crumbs form. Add the shredded coconut
    and stir until well combined.

4   Spread the crumble mixture evenly over the
    berries. Bake for 25–30 minutes, until golden.
    Serve with ice-cream.

Working on this cookbook has been a joy for me –
speaking to farmers across the country and sharing
their stories of life on the land has been inspiring.
As managing editor, I was happy to see so many of
my fellow writers and editors offer their services to
support such a good cause. Many even thanked me
for the opportunity to help. The food media community
in Australia is small but incredibly talented and such a
generous community. I feel privileged to be part of it.

   In the spirit of family and giving, here is my family's recipe for chocolate
fudge cupcakes, affectionately known as Nanna cakes. My mother, Elaine
has perfected this recipe over the years and brings them to every family
gathering. They always bring a smile to my face (and the faces of the
children) when they are served. **LYNNE TESTONI**

nanna cakes

MAKES 24

60G BUTTER, SOFTENED

1 CUP (220G) SUGAR

1 EGG

1 TEASPOON VANILLA EXTRACT

1½ CUPS (225G) SELF-RAISING FLOUR

1 TABLESPOON COCOA POWDER

½ CUP (125ML) MILK

¼ CUP (60ML) BOILING WATER

HUNDREDS AND THOUSANDS,
   TO DECORATE

CHOCOLATE ICING

1 CUP (125G) ICING SUGAR, SIFTED

1 TABLESPOON COCOA POWDER

30G BUTTER, SOFTENED

1–2 TABLESPOONS BOILING WATER

1   Preheat the oven to 180°C. Line two 12-hole
    patty pan trays (2 tablespoon capacity) with
    paper cases.

2   Using an electric mixer, beat the softened
    butter, sugar, egg and vanilla for 2 minutes,
    until pale and creamy. Gently fold in the sifted
    flour and cocoa in alternating batches with the
    milk and boiling water until smooth.

3   Divide the batter among the paper cases and
    bake for 12–15 minutes, until firm to the touch.
    Cool the cakes in the tins for 5 minutes before
    transferring to a wire rack to cool completely.

4   To make the icing, stir the icing sugar, cocoa,
    butter and boiling water together until thick
    and smooth, a little adding extra boiling water
    if necessary.

5   Spread the icing over the cooled cakes and
    sprinkle with hundreds and thousands. Place
    on a wire rack to set.

ACKNOWLEDGEMENTS

So, so, so many people to thank and there could never be enough space to adequately express my sincere gratitude to each and everyone of them. It has been so heartwarming to witness how willing all the people who worked on *Farmer* were to give so freely of their time for such a great cause. A lot of the people who contributed their time were from the food publishing industry and they know firsthand the value of what farmers do. Without them we would not have jobs. It has been a total honour to have helped mother *Farmer* into the world. I truly hope you love her as much as we do. Take the time to read her heartfelt stories and cook her truly treasured family recipes. Know that by purchasing this book you are making a difference, and I thank you for that.

Without the following people, *Farmer* would not have been possible. Deep gratitude to each and every one of you.

THE CORE TEAM
Many, many late nights for these wonderful big-hearted folks who showed up day in, day out after work and spent hours bringing *Farmer* to life: Odette Barry, Hannah Brady, Lynne Testoni, Justine Harding.

DESIGN
Hieu Nguyen, who is responsible for the look and feel of this gorgeous book, and who gave an insane amount of hours pulling it all together. We are so appreciative of your contribution, knowledge and experience.
Hannah Brady, who got the ball rolling and worked tirelessly stalking photographers, organising photo shoots and gathering images.

PHOTOGRAPHERS
To all of the photographers who shot our beautiful recipe images and farmers, your images have made this book truly stunning. I need to make mention of a few photographers who went above and beyond, jumped in their cars and drove far and wide to shoot our farmer stories: Scott Hawkins, Kathy Mexted, Vanessa Levis, Oliver Ford.
Thank you to Geoff Boccolati for allowing us to use his studio and to Mickey Robertson at Glenmore House for having us there to shoot recipes. Thank you also to all of the other photographers who opened their studios to us. Thank you to Wendy Sheehan for her gorgeous drone photographs.

RECIPE PHOTOGRAPHERS
Joe Filshie, Oliver Ford, Luisa Brimble, Scott Hawkins, Pablo Martin, Jeremy Simons, Cath Muscat, Nicky Ryan, Amanda Bate, Nic Gossage.

FARMER PHOTOGRAPHERS
Andrea Mitchell, Amber Winzer, Kara Rosenlund, Jane Smith, Wendy Sheehan, Wendy Johnston, Kate Holmes, Nelly Le Comte, Jeremy Simons, Luisa Brimble, Sally Chilicott, Tara Lee, Julia Foyster, Gemma Gers.

COVER PHOTOGRAPHY
Thank you to Jane Smith for the beautiful image of her daughter Annabelle.

FOOD EDITORS
Compiling a book with 80 different recipes from people with a wide range of recipe writing experience is a big task. These women helped pull the recipes into shape: Anneka Manning, Tracy Rutherford, Cathie Lonnie, Darlene Allston, Jennene Plummer, Amira Georgy, Michelle Southan, Miranda Payne.

EDITORS
Led by the amazing mover and shaker, Lynne Testoni, who managed our team of editors and writers who pinned down farmers for interviews and polished up the recipes.
Justine Harding, who calmly and graciously brought it all together into one homogeneous collection of recipes and stories. You have the patience of a saint, my sweet trustworthy and reliable friend. Thanks for saving my bacon, literally.
Penny Carroll, Lyn Justice, Kylie Walker, Justine Harding.

WRITERS
Elizabeth Jurman, Sally Wilson, Tracey Platt, Ylla Wright, Kathy Mexted, Nicole Conville, John Burfitt, Rachel Smith, Penny Carroll, Rebecca Cox, Leigh Livingstone, David Smiedt Samera Kamaleddine, Bec Hanley, Tricha Tippapart, Kim Berry.

PROPS
Props are a very costly part of a cookbook. We were incredibly fortunate to have two of Sydney's biggest prop houses donate all of the props for this book. Thank you to Georgie from Major and Tom, and Georgie at Prop CoOp.
Thanks to Akubra for their generous donation of hats.
To the ceramicists who donated their props for us to use in the book and to auction at our fundraiser, thank you so much.
@cone11ceramics
@madeofaustralia
@karenwalker
@katherinemahoneyceramics
@girlnomad
@marieheleneclauzon
@penelopeduke
@bisukettostudio
@shedevlin
@nicceramics
@jenbettyeverett
@derum
@gd_clay
@claybeehive
@frankvoid
@littlecharliewheeler
@claycanoe

STYLISTS AND HOME ECS/FOOD PREP

Our stylists and home ecs/food prep teams did such a stellar job of making the food in this book look so damn delicious. The food images are stunning and beg you to cook the recipes. I would like to make special mention of Anneka Manning for her support and extra recipe testing and writing. Thanks also to Georgie Dolling and photographer Joe Filshie, who jumped on board from the get go and did everything they could to help us out in any way they could.

STYLISTS

Olivia Blackmore, Georgie Dolling, Kirsten Jenkins, Kristen Wilson, Yael Grinham, Janelle Bloom, Jane Collins, Steve Pearce, Lucy Tweed, Kate Murdoch, Hannah Brady.

FOOD PREP

Theressa Klein, Peta Dent, Wendy Quisumbing, Grace Campbell, Warren Mendes, Melissa Hurwitz, Annie Logue, Mandy Sinclair, Jane Ash, Rita Ince, Karen Buckley, Jess Brooks, Margaret Sevenjhazi, Georgie Esdaile, Samantha Coutts, Sarah Jane Hallett.

RECIPE CONTRIBUTORS

We have had recipes given to us by famous chefs, farmers, professional recipe writers and home cooks and we are thankful for each and every one. Sophie Hansen, Jeff McMullen, Hayden Quinn, Greg Cromwell, Jane Grover, Warren Mendes, Jason Roberts, Wendy Johnston, Julia Foyster, Shane Hickey, Sam Grima, Fraser Bayley, Mickey Robertson, Matt Moran, Kirsten Jenkins, Chezzi & Grant Denyer, Ronni Kahn, Erica Dibden, Beau Cook, Sally Kaptein, Janelle Bloom, Maggie Beer, Hetty McKinnon, Sonja Bernyk, Wayne Adams, Annette Forrest, Michelle Bridges, Paul Dawson, Tony Poyner, Janet Mitchell, Amber Winzer, Jane Grylls, Martin Boetz, Stephanie Alexander, Matt Preston, Jamie Oliver, Julie & Jeremy Shaw, Matt Stone, Dr Libby Weaver, Yasmine O'Sullivan, Andrea Mitchell, Bec Duffy, Erika Watson, Richard Fairley, Beverley Laing, David Chung, Anna Phillips, Sarah Mayoh, Steve Jackson, Becky Searles, Anna Jewell, Morag Gamble, Matt Wilkinson, Mitzi Westang, Jane Smith, Phoebe Wood, Sarah Swan, Nadine Ingram, Darlene Allston, Steve Webber, Sheryl Rennie, Darren Robertson, Anneka Manning, Odette Barry, Cathie Lonnie, Emma Dean, Lucy Lewis, Gillian Leeds, Belinda Jeffery, Didie Griffin, Michelle Southan, Courtney Young, Lyndey Milan, Sally Empringham, Roslyn Anderson, Dan Walker, Wendy Sheehan, Jody Vassallo, Lisa Elias, Lynne Testoni.

FARMERS

Our farmers are what this book is about. Thank you for letting us into your lives and sharing your stories with us: Tim & Sophie Hansen, Greg Cromwell, Shane Hickey, Sam & Steve Grima, Erica & Nick Dibden, Paul Dawson and the BackTrack crew, Amber Winzer & Jason Wright, David & Andrea Mitchell, Erika Watson & Hayden Druce, Richard Fairley, David Chung, Anna Jewell, Mitzi Westang, Jane Smith, Steve Webber, Gillian Leeds, Courtney Young & Ian Congdon, Dan Walker, Helen Elias.

INDEXERS AND PROOFREADERS

To Andree and the folks at Puddingburn who so kindly said yes when I cold-called them and asked for their help with this book.

COURIERS

Thank you Vlad Ivanovic Couriers for delivering and returning props all over Sydney.

MARKETING, PR AND CROWDFUNDING

Odette & Co did an incredible job steering this ship and continue to do so. Their tireless efforts with social media meant that *Farmer* got radio, TV and print exposure, and raised awareness of our Chuffed crowdfunding campaign.

SALES DISTRIBUTION

Sue Brockoff and the team at Harper Collins who were so supportive of *Farmer* from the first email. Thank you for warehousing her and for getting her in front of trade retailers and then out into stores.

ADVICE AND SUPPORT

Beth Drumm, for the time you spent with me on the phone discussing this book. Kay Richardson, your advice and support about crowdfunding has been invaluable.

PRINTING

Robert Stapelfeldt at Ligare, you have been a total legend you went above and beyond in getting us a reduced print cost, great paper stock and producing a fantastic-looking book delivered on time. Also Syd Geary, who printed our posters for marketing material, Signarama for our pull-up banners and Bangalow Sign Company for our marquee signage. To Vanessa and her team at Print Made Easy, Narooma, who kindly printed the *Farmer* Christmas gift vouchers.

OTHER

Rebecca Searles for her tireless work with the gorgeous *Farmer* cookbook video and song. Miranda O'Rourke, Harrison Balodis and the team at Parterre Garden for all their fundraising efforts. All of the folks who donated items for our fundraising auction. And to all these other folks who gave us help with in one way or another, from donations, finding farmers, chefs, recipes, retouching, equipment hire, donating their time to this wonderful cause, thank you: Gourmet Garden, Harry and Kristof from Akropol fruit and veg, Richard Luxton, Yvonne Huntley, Jane Grylls, Luisa Brimble, Kirsten Jenkins, Warren Mendes, Bill Wilson, Sue Dodd, Kim Jansen.

I also need to thank the people who supported us online and pre-purchased copies of the book to help us raise funds for printing. That was a huge leap of faith you took for us and it was instrumental in getting us to this point.

RECIPE INDEX

CONVERSION CHART

1 METRIC TABLESPOON = 20ML • 1 METRIC TEASPOON = 5ML • 1 CUP = 250ML (8 FL OZ)

TEMPERATURE CONVERSIONS

°C (Celcius)	Gas Mark	°F (Fahrenheit)
120	1	250
150	2	300
160	3	325
180	4	350
200	5	400
220	6	450
240	7	500

LIQUID MEASURES

Metric (Millilitres)	Imperial (Fluid ounces)
30ml	1 fl oz
60ml	2 fl oz
90ml	3 fl oz
125ml	4 fl oz
150ml	5 fl oz
180ml	6 fl oz
200ml	7 fl oz
250ml	8 fl oz
280ml	9 fl oz
310ml	10 fl oz
340ml	11 fl oz
375ml	12 fl oz
500ml	16 fl oz
1 litre	32 fl oz

DRY MEASURES

Metric (Grams)	Imperial (Ounces/Pounds)
30g	1oz
60g	2oz
90g	3oz
125g	4oz
150g	5oz
180g	6oz
200g	7oz
250g	8oz
280g	9oz
310g	10oz
340g	11oz
375g	12oz
500g	16oz/1lb
1kg	32oz/2lb

LENGTH CONVERSIONS

Centimetres (cm) Millimeters (mm)	Inches (in)
2–3mm	⅛in
5–6mm	¼in
1cm	½in
2cm	¾in
2.5cm	1in
5cm	2in
6cm	2½in
8cm	3in
10cm	4in
13cm	5in
15cm	6in
18cm	7in
20cm	8in
23cm	9in
25cm	10in
28cm	11in
30cm	12in

First published 2019. Reprinted 2019.
First Australian Paperback Edition 2019
ISBN 978-0-9942406-6-8

Farmer cookbook
© Jody Vassallo 2019

Published by
Jody Vassallo Pty Ltd
Latimers Lane
Central Tilba NSW 2546
AUSTRALIA
Email: foodbyjodyv@yahoo.com
Phone: 0414 559 889

Printed and bound in Australia by
Ligare Printers

Sales and distribution by
HarperCollins Publishers Australia
Level 13, 201 Elizabeth Street
Sydney NSW 2000
AUSTRALIA
Phone: 02 9952 5000